Dún na nGall, 'Fort of the Foreigners'?

Maynooth Studies in Local History

SERIES EDITOR Michael Potterton

The six volumes in the MSLH series for 2024 cover a broad chronological and geographical canvas across four provinces, focusing variously on people, places, families, communities and events. It begins with an unlikely search for Vikings in the north-west of Ireland, where the evidence is more compelling than most people realize. Further south, in Carrick-on-Shannon, we trace the fortunes of the St George family from the Plantation of Leitrim through to the decades after the Famine. From Carrick we continue south to Ballymurray in Roscommon and its Quaker community (1717–1848), including their relationship with the Croftons of Mote Park. Further south still, in 1701 Jacobite Patrick Hurly of Moughna, Co. Clare, was at the centre of a 'sham robbery' of gold and jewellery worth about €500,000 in today's money. Unlike Hurly, Mary Mercer was renowned for her charitable endeavours, including the establishment of a shelter for orphaned girls in Dublin three hundred years ago in 1724. Finally, the last volume in this year's crop examines the evolution of the resilient farming community at Carbury in Co. Kildare.

* * *

Raymond Gillespie passed away after a very short illness on 8 February 2024. He had established the Maynooth Studies in Local History (MSLH) series with Irish Academic Press in 1995, from which time he served as series editor for a remarkable 27 years and 153 volumes. Taking over those editorial reins in 2021, my trepidation was tempered by the knowledge that Raymond agreed to remain as an advisor. True to his word, he continued to recommend contributors, provide peer-review, mentor first-time authors (and series editors) and give sound advice. Shoes that seemed big to fill in 2021 just got a lot bigger.

Maynooth Studies in Local History: Number 169

Dún na nGall, 'Fort of the Foreigners'? The Vikings and their legacy in Donegal

Megan McAuley

FOUR COURTS PRESS

Set in 11.5pt on 13.5pt Bembo by
Carrigboy Typesetting Services for
FOUR COURTS PRESS LTD
7 Malpas Street, Dublin 8, Ireland
www.fourcourtspress.ie
and in North America for
FOUR COURTS PRESS
c/o IPG, 814 N Franklin Street, Chicago, IL 60610

© Megan McAuley and Four Courts Press 2024

ISBN 978-1-80151-132-2

All rights reserved. Without limiting the rights under copyright reserved alone, no part of this publication may be reproduced, stored in or introduced into a retrieval system, or transmitted, in any form or by any means (electronic, mechanical, photocopying, recording or otherwise), without the prior written permission of both the copyright owner and the above publisher of this book.

Printed in Ireland
by Sprint Books, Dublin

Contents

Acknowledgments		6
Introduction		7
1	Archaeological evidence for Vikings in Co. Donegal	14
2	Documentary evidence for Vikings in Co. Donegal	32
3	Viking legacies in Donegal	49
Conclusion		67
Notes		71
Abbreviations		71
Index		80

FIGURES

1	Silver arm-rings from 'north-west Inishowen'	15
2	Raphoe hoard, showing ingots and arm-rings	18
3	Inscription on stone at Carrowmore	20
4	Carrowmore hoard, showing arm-rings	21
5	Hoard of arm-rings from Roosky	23
6	Silver ring-money from Lurgabrack	26
7	Medieval house at Rinnaraw	28
8	Map of evidence for Vikings in Donegal	68

TABLES

1	Old Norse loanwords found in Irish	51
2	Norse-influenced place-names in Ireland	58
3	Folkloric evidence for Vikings in Donegal	61

Acknowledgments

I would like to sincerely thank Michael Potterton, who supervised the thesis that became this book, for his invaluable encouragement, guidance and support over the last number of years. His excellent editorship and diligence have made writing this contribution for the Maynooth Studies in Local History series very enjoyable, and an opportunity for which I am most grateful. I am very thankful to all those who answered my questions and shared their extensive knowledge with me when I began researching Vikings in Donegal a number of years ago, including Richard Warner, Brian Lacey, Charles Doherty, Caroline Carr (Donegal Museum) and Sean Beattie. Thank you to all of my friends and family for their constant encouragement, especially my parents, Pauline and Joe, for their support, patience and love. *Go raibh maith agaibhse go léir.*

Introduction

Dún na nGall, from which the anglicized name of 'Donegal' comes, is composed of the words *dún*, meaning 'fort', and *gall*, 'foreigner'.[1] *Dún na nGall* therefore translates as 'Fort of the Foreigners'. There has been much academic speculation on who or what group is being referred to, as potentially the term could indicate Vikings, Normans, Anglo-Normans, English or any other group that could be considered 'foreign' in a Gaelic land. Further study of the terms *dún* and *gall* support the theory that the 'foreigners' were Vikings. *Dún*, according to Niall Ó Dónaill's *Foclóir Gaeilge-Bearla*, is a 'fortress', 'secure residence' or 'stronghold', while *gall* can describe a 'foreigner', 'Northman' or 'Dane'.[2] This study argues that the 'foreigners' in question were Vikings by compiling evidence of Viking activity in Co. Donegal and by considering the Viking legacy in the county. The majority of research undertaken on the Viking Age in Ireland concerns Dublin and the south-east of the country. This study challenges the notion that Scandinavian settlement during this period was exclusively focused on the southern half of the island. To consider the case for Donegal, evidence from a range of disciplines will be examined, including history, archaeology, onomastics, linguistics and folklore.

VIKING ORIGINS

'Vikings' are defined as Scandinavian seafaring pirates and traders who raided and settled in parts of north-western Europe from the eighth to the eleventh century.[3] Most of the Vikings that came to Ireland are thought to have originated in western Norway, reaching this country via the Western Isles of Scotland and the North Channel.[4] The first recorded Viking attack in 795, on *Rechru* or *Rechrainn*, is commonly believed to have been on Rathlin Island.[5] This, and the subsequent attacks on Inishmurray and Inishbofin, could all have

7

been accomplished by one original exploratory crew.[6] Howth (*c.*821), Skellig Michael (*c.*824), Glendalough, Derry, Clondalkin (*c.*830s) and others were hit in the early stages of Viking pillage. Historians suspect that these raids were not the first contact between the Irish and the Vikings, however, and have speculated that their arrival in Ireland began with small-scale settlements and trade links connecting Ireland with Europe. Moreover, those trading contacts may have occurred generations before the violent raids described in contemporary texts: 'How did the Vikings know where all those monasteries were? [...] there was already contact. They were already trading before those raids happened'.[7] By the mid-ninth century, the Vikings were using the river systems and lakes to penetrate the heart of the country, at which time they entered a second period of temporary settlement: overwintering. The Vikings established *longphorts* (Kilmainham-Islandbridge, Annagassan, Woodstown, Lough Ree, Dunrally), which later became the basis for the third phase, permanent settlement, in Dublin, Wexford, Waterford, Cork and Limerick.

The Vikings in Irish history had previously been subject to misinterpretation, stereotyped as a ruthless band of pagan warriors only interested in pillaging:

> Vikings were [considered] inveterate plunderers and psychopathic thugs who terrorized the Irish, and Irish monks in particular, until that outsize heroic figure, Brian Bóruma, denied them their conquest of Ireland by his noble victory at Clontarf in 1014.[8]

The definition of the word 'Viking' itself has been manipulated to portray different activities, conducted by disparate people, such as: attacking, plundering and raiding; colonizing and settling; and bartering and trading. The first phase of these activities stems from the Old Norse *víkingr*, a sea-robber who was traditionally associated with the *vikr* or inlets of Norway. Vikings, in this limited definition of seafaring piracy, existed long before the true beginnings of the Viking Age, and were the most overtly violent manifestation of the definition, the brutal image of which became firmly embedded in Irish cultural history.[9] Recent historiography has argued that medieval propaganda literature (such as *Cogadh Gaedhel re Gallaibh*, a

Introduction 9

hyperbolic tale written by the descendants of Brian Bóruma) helped to solidify this stereotype, and that the coming of the Vikings to Ireland actually had positive consequences. Excavations at Dublin, and subsequently in other settlements of Viking origin, have shown that Viking centres of trade grew into towns during the tenth century. From this, it has been argued that urbanism was introduced by the Vikings to Irish society, even though they had no towns, by definition, in the Scandinavian homelands when they first arrived.[10] Charles Doherty argued that 'we should not underestimate the very real power of the Norse, and their physical and psychological impact on Irish people'.[11] Cultural interaction and interchange became key features of Viking-Age Ireland from the tenth century onwards, though the country never experienced extensive and intensive rural colonization by Vikings such as occurred in Scotland, England and Normandy.[12]

* * *

Chapter 1 explores the wide range of archaeological evidence for Viking activity in Donegal. A collection of silver arm-rings likely imported by Vikings was discovered at Carrowmore in 1932 and a second silver hoard was unearthed at Roosky in 1966.[13] Locals believed that a 'Dane' was buried at the cashel with an internal souterrain in Roosky, but it was not until almost twenty years after this folktale was recorded that four Viking silver arm-rings were discovered, hidden in the wall of the cashel.[14] A collection of Viking silver arm-rings was found in 'north-west Inishowen' and a silver ingot located near Dunfanaghy.[15] A probable Viking hoard of tenth-century Anglo-Saxon coins was discovered in the mid-nineteenth century near Burt.[16] A hoard of four silver ingots, six silver arm-rings and one earring of Viking origin was found in the vicinity of Raphoe.[17] A ringed pin of Irish-Viking type, recovered from the beach at Kinnegar strand, is likely associated with a Viking burial, as Richard Warner speculated that the sand dunes at Kinnegar were the location of a Viking cemetery.[18] At Rinnaraw, on the western side of Sheephaven Bay (a place-name with possible Old Norse origins), a coastal cashel was excavated which unearthed a medieval house. The house, dating to around the ninth century, was compared to similar Viking examples with rounded external corners in the Orkneys.[19] Whetstones recovered at Rinnaraw were likened to examples found in excavations of Viking Dublin. More recent discoveries have also been made, such as the hoard of eight silver arm-rings unearthed at Lurgaback, Horn Head, in 2011.[20]

Chapter 1 uses historical archaeology to investigate the physical evidence for Viking activity in Donegal. This combines two distinct, but interconnected, disciplines: archaeology and history. Although archaeology and history differ widely in terms of approach, raw materials and method, both disciplines deal with the study of human lives in the past.[21] David Percy Dymond describes the advantages of an archaeological history methodological approach: 'If documentary and physical evidence both exist for a certain subject, then surely a co-ordinated study must be nearer the [...] truth than a simple documentary or archaeological treatment'.[22] The archaeologist is concerned with artefacts, ranging from small objects to the physical environment, while the historian is concerned with writings.[23] Archaeological history, therefore, combines archaeological evidence with written evidence to establish the broadest possible understanding from all of the available sources. The archaeological evidence of Vikings in Donegal is then considered in the context of the historical evidence.

* * *

Chapter 2 assesses the documentary sources that illuminate the extent of Viking activity and/or settlement in Donegal. The Annals of Ulster, the Annals of the Four Masters and *Chronicon Scotorum* (aka *Chronicum Scotorum*) are explored with this focus.[24] An example of bardic poetry may highlight how Vikings fit into the political narrative in Donegal in the ninth century. The poem *Ard na scéala, a mheic na ccuach* (ascribed to Flann MacLónain), a eulogy to Éichnechán, the lord of Fanad, describes the events surrounding the marriages of Éichnechán's three daughters to the Vikings Cathais, Tuirgeis and Galltor, and subsequent battles between the native Irish and the Norsemen.[25] Carrickabraghy, mentioned in this poem as the location where Cathais, Tuirgeis and Galltor settled with the daughters of

Éichnechán, may have been a Viking base. As monastic sites were attractive to Viking raiders during the first phase of their activity in Ireland, sources relating to early ecclesiastical settlements are examined to uncover information about Viking raids on such sites.

The historian must be cautious when interpreting the annals and literature pertaining to monastic sites, due to the potential for religious bias and exaggeration. Furthermore, annalistic sources are not particularly detailed, in both language and content, as noted by Radner:

> Typically, adjectives and adverbs are lacking, the range of vocabulary is severely limited, and the language of the entries is mainly formulaic. The range of events reported is almost as constrained as the language of reportage. Major natural disasters. Natural deaths of kings, lay nobility, high-ranking churchmen, scholars. Slayings and assassinations of the same sorts of personnel. Raids and battles.[26]

Within the annals, there are few statements of opinion, evaluation or suggestions as to cause or effect.[27] The historian must be careful not to assume too much. Annals are nonetheless an invaluable source when stripped back and properly cross-checked. Bardic poetry is at risk of containing inherent bias and exaggeration, as the chronicler or bard has been commissioned to write a poem, usually glorifying a member of his patron family. Bardic poetry was intended to be publicly recited as entertainment during a feast, usually describing past familial legacies and the patron's present political ambitions, hopes and fears. Poetry is still valuable as a historical source, 'although the evidence it provides must be interpreted with due regard for the literary conventions within which it is composed'.[28] In documentary sources that have been transcribed, there may be mistranslations or scribal errors. The best way to avoid bias in this regard is to cross-check a number of translated sources. One such example of mistranslation or misinterpretation is the word *longphort*, which was initially employed to specifically describe a Viking overwintering camp (which sometimes became permanent) and was later adopted into Irish to describe any fortified camp, or stronghold, not necessarily related to Vikings.[29]

* * *

Chapter 3 considers the legacy left by the Vikings in Donegal. Toponymical sources are investigated as a number of place-names, particularly in the Inishowen area, show evidence for the presence of Vikings. In Tullagh, Clonmany, for example, there was a place called 'Norway'. While this place-name is no longer in use, evidence of its former existence is found on Ordnance Survey maps and in marriage records from the nineteenth century.[30] More examples of Old Norse-influenced or Viking-related place-names are discussed in this chapter. Old Norse also had a significant impact on the Irish language. It may have influenced the Ulster Irish dialect, *Gaeilge Uladh*. For example, *Luchter*, an Ulster Irish word for a handful, is understood to come from the Norse *lagthr*, meaning a handful of wool.[31] Additionally, this chapter deals with the emergence and subsequent legacy of the Gall-Ghaedhil (Norse-Gael), the descendants of intermarriage between Vikings and native Irish. A study of surnames in Donegal establishes possible patterns of Norse-Gael migration, marriage and settlement. Finally, the longstanding Viking legacy evident in Donegal's oral culture is considered through a selection of folktales gathered from the National Folklore Collection.

Seán Mac Labhraí argues that 'history holds the explanation as to why the majority of place-names in Ireland cannot be immediately understood nowadays'.[32] This is mostly due to different groups of people expanding their influence across Ireland, including Celts, Romans, Vikings, Normans and so on. Thus, place-names can be clues for the archaeologist, as they are fossils of human geography.[33] The role of *dinnshenchus* (lore of famous places) in early Irish literature places the study of Irish place-names as an essential, integral part of Irish culture, stretching back through medieval times.[34] Methodologically, 'there are two basic ways to conduct toponymic research – one concentrating on the etymology, meaning and origin of toponyms, and one focusing on the toponyms of a region and examining patterns of these names'.[35] Norse-influenced place-names, and surnames, that are common in Donegal are investigated. Surname analysis, like toponymy, can be challenging due to poor handwriting, spelling variations and errors in transcriptions, but in the interest of avoiding bias, it is necessary to consider all occurrences of a name with all possible alternatives.

Introduction

To summarize, this book considers that the *gall* ('foreigners') in *Dún na nGall* ('Fort of the Foreigners') were Vikings. This multidisciplinary study uses sources from history, archaeology, onomastics, linguistics and folklore to collate evidence for the presence of Vikings in Donegal. The extent of Viking activity and/or settlement in Donegal over the three known phases (plundering, overwintering, permanent settlement) is considered throughout. This highlights the impact that Vikings had on the cultural, linguistic and political landscape of Donegal during this period, and the Viking legacy that survives in oral culture.

1. Archaeological evidence for Vikings in Co. Donegal

The earliest find of Viking silver, uncovered at an unspecified location in north-west Inishowen, also happens to be the largest hoard found in Donegal. This is the only known archaeological evidence for Vikings discovered during the eighteenth century. In the nineteenth century, a hoard of Anglo-Saxon coins was found during the construction of the Derry to Letterkenny railway. The majority of the archaeological evidence was unearthed during the twentieth and twenty-first centuries, such as the silver hoard found at Raphoe, at the turn of the century, followed by the Carrowmore and Roosky hoards. The most recent find is the Lurgabrack ring-money hoard, found in 2011, which is significant for both its contents and its location. The excavation of one site will be analysed: the remains of a medieval dwelling found within a cashel at Rinnaraw, which shows striking similarities to Viking houses excavated on the Orkneys. Lastly, a few finds and sites for which there is very little published information are briefly mentioned, including a potential ingot hoard at Liss, an ingot fragment from Clondahorky and a Viking ringed-pin found on the shores of Kinnegar beach.[1]

'NORTH-WEST INISHOWEN'

Little is known of the earliest discovered and, to this day, largest Viking-age silver hoard from Co. Donegal. The hoard was found c.1790 in north-west Inishowen, and there is no information regarding the circumstances of the find. The only documentary evidence is the following, reproduced by James Graham-Campbell:

> part of a group lately found in the northwest side of Ennishowen, in the county of Donegal. The group consisted of nine or ten of the narrow double rings, hanging within the broad single

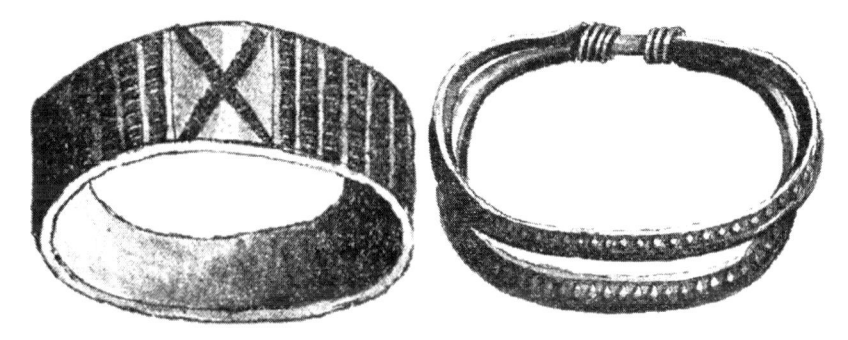

1. Two silver arm-rings from the 'north-west Inishowen' hoard
(source: Graham-Campbell, 'The Viking-Age silver hoards of Ireland', p. 50)

one; each of the double rings nearly resembling one another; differing only a little about the twisted parts, and in the form of the ornament on the circumference. Five only of the double rings, with the single one, remain; the other four or five having been wrought up by the silver smith who purchased them.[2]

The weight of the entire hoard can be estimated at 500g.[3] A sketch made of two of the silver arm-rings (fig. 1) may be mistaken in depicting the 'broad single' ring of Hiberno-Viking type as annular, on the grounds that 'it is hard to envisage how the double rings could have been hung within the single ring unless it was penannular [...] it should be noted that all other known rings of this type [...] are penannular in form'.[4]

In other respects, however, the drawing accurately depicts the size and appearance of two Viking silver arm-rings of ninth- to tenth-century date, such as those in the collection of Hiberno-Viking and double arm-rings in the National Museum of Ireland.[5] It has been suggested, given the similarity of the Inishowen arm-rings to other examples (such as Raphoe, Carrowmore and Roosky, to follow), that the deposition date was c.950 to 1050, highlighted by the common feature of at least one Hiberno-Viking ring in each.[6] There was no mention of the Inishowen hoard in the *Transactions of the Royal Irish Academy* published in the 1790s, or in the minutes of the Committee of Antiquities of the Royal Irish Academy (May 1785 to June 1850), thus, it is unlikely that 'the illustrated Inishowen rings ever entered the Academy's collection and so their fate remains unknown'.[7]

CARROWEN, BURT

A hoard of five Anglo-Saxon pennies was found in Carrowen, a townland in Burt, during the construction of the railway from Derry to Letterkenny *c*.1864.[8] More were discovered, but only five were kept by the finders. Michael Dolley reinterprets the entry in J.D.A. Thompson's *Inventory of British coin hoards*, in which the suspected deposition date for the coins was *c*.905:

> Since the hoard contains coins of Eadgar who did not succeed Eadwig until the autumn of 959, the deposition date 905 is absurd. Even if we were to accept that Eadgar had struck coins in his own name during the secession of 957–959, it would be hard to date the Irish hoard before *c*.960, and one feels that most numismatists would incline to a date *c*.965.[9]

What was believed to be a 'second parcel from the same hoard' of six Anglo-Saxon pennies is described in Thompson's *Inventory* as being found at Lough Swilly in 1864 and the likely date of deposition *c*.950 to 970.[10] Again, it was argued that no hoard of Eadgar coins could be found in Ireland earlier than *c*.960. Both hoards were composed exclusively of coins of Eadgar and only *BM Cat*. Types I and III were represented. All the coins described appear to have originated from north-eastern England, with Adelaver, Grid, Unbein and Farthein striking at Lincoln. The coins of Asferth and Isembert clearly derived from the same region, and Herolf was a moneyer of York. There is an apparent absence of coins from north-western England, even given the small sample size.[11]

The second hoard also came from the parish of Burt, and was found during the construction of the Letterkenny railway.[12] Strangely, Thompson's *Inventory* map rejects the original account and instead indicates that this second hoard was found west of Lough Swilly (Burt is to the east). Dolley believed that the two hoards of identical deposition date, both found during construction of the Letterkenny railway, were likely found in the same place, 'the more so because the west of Ulster lies outside the area where Viking-Age hoards usually occur'.[13] Lough Swilly is one of only three glacial fjords in Ireland and, as we know that Vikings were documented there (according to a

Archaeological evidence for Vikings in Co. Donegal 17

number of references in the annals), it is not impossible that two hoards of Anglo-Saxon pennies were discovered during the construction of the railway. Interestingly, there was a long-standing folk belief in the local area that treasure was concealed at the find-spot.[14]

'NEAR RAPHOE'

At the turn of the twentieth century, *c.*1903, a hoard of Viking-Age silver arm-rings and ingots was discovered 'at the base of a drystone ditch' near Raphoe, south-west of the Inishowen Peninsula.[15] It was not until decades later, in July 1979, that the silver hoard came to public attention, when it was published in *Sotheby's Sale Catalogue* and subsequently sold to an anonymous purchaser. Graham-Campbell's attempts to contact the unknown vendor and purchaser were in vain, but he was allowed to examine the hoard by a director of Sotheby's Antiquities Department prior to the auction.[16] The Raphoe silver hoard consisted of four ingots, six arm-rings and part of a seventh (fig. 2). The four ingots were all of sub-rectangular form and cross-section. Four out of the six arm-rings were penannular, varying in external diameter from *c.*7.6 to 9.4cm. The final two arm-rings were non-penannular, one consisting of a plain rod of silver with lozenge-shaped cross-section while the other was plain with a circular cross-section which forms one-and-a-half spirals.[17] The final piece in the hoard was an arm-ring fragment, similar in form to the non-penannular arm-rings aforementioned. Graham-Campbell negated the description by Sotheby's that this was a penannular earring, arguing that 'the wearing of earrings was an Eastern fashion that never became established amongst the Scandinavians during the Viking period'.[18]

As very little information is recoverable about the Raphoe hoard, it is difficult to decide on a potential deposition date. The two plain closed rings are too simple to provide any chronological clues. The ring with one-and-a-half spirals is similar to both the decorated double rings and the plain single rings of common occurrence, while the bigger ring is also paralleled in Ireland.[19] One closed ring from the Raphoe hoard does have chronological significance, despite its simplicity and lack of ornamentation. This type of plain penannular

2. The Raphoe hoard, showing ingots, arm-rings and arm-ring fragment
(source: Graham-Campbell, 'A Viking-Age silver hoard from near Raphoe', p. 109, pl. 1)

ring, known as 'ring-money', appears to date to between the early tenth century and the late eleventh century and forms an important element in Viking-Age silver hoards of Scotland.[20] Other examples of ring-money are known from Ireland, such as that found at Horn Head in 2011. The Raphoe fragment may have been cut from a piece of ring-money, or from a closed ring, but it was 'presumably cut to a specific weight for a particular purpose for which it was bent into a circle' to be used in a monetary context.[21]

One example of a coin-dated hoard that contains arm-rings of both the Hiberno-Norse and ring-money types was found at Grimestad, Norway, and for which the given deposition date is c.930.[22] Consequently, the Grimestad hoard provides a potential deposition date for the Raphoe hoard. This date is corroborated by the fact that Hiberno-Norse rings are not known from any later hoard and that ring-money was not present in any earlier hoard. The Raphoe and Grimestad hoards therefore belong to a brief period in which both types of arm-ring were in circulation together, c.920 to 940. Graham-Campbell believed that 'the Raphoe hoard was almost certainly deposited in the 920s or 930s'.[23] This date range coincides with references in the annals to a Viking presence in Inishowen, which will be discussed in Chapter 2. Another silver hoard from Scandinavia that shows parallels with the Raphoe hoard is the Bøstrand hoard, also from Norway. The Bøstrand hoard was likewise coinless, consisting of eleven arm-rings and four fragments, including rings of ornamented Hiberno-Viking type, closed rings and one example of ring-money, similar to that in the Raphoe hoard.[24] It is probable that the Raphoe hoard is of a similar date to the Bøstrand and Grimestad hoards and, furthermore, it provides evidence of the links between Norway and the Norse settlements in Ireland at this time.[25]

CARROWMORE, QUIGLEY'S POINT

Five silver arm-rings were discovered at Carrowmore in 1933. Quarrymen were working near the village of Quigley's Point and, 'while engaged on the removal of a large stone, they came upon a series of silver bracelets beneath it'.[26] Quigley's Point is a small village on the Inishowen shore of Lough Foyle. On this high land there were the remains of several megalithic graves, some of which were unrecorded, according to Sean P. Ó Ríordáin, and on the summit was a stone-built enclosure.[27] The large stone under which the arm-rings were discovered was composed of chlorite schist and was covered by soil cleared by the quarrymen. They described the arm-rings as having been 'enveloped, when found, in a ball of a substance like clay, and they were linked in order of size, but were found "bunched together" and not extended'.[28]

Five arm-rings were found but two were broken and the fragments lost. An excavation conducted subsequently revealed no trace of a grave at the location, and the only other object discovered was some fragmentary iron. A series of incised markings were noticed (fig. 3)

3. Unconfirmed inscription on the large stone at Carrowmore under which a Viking silver hoard was discovered (source: Ó Ríordáin, 'Recent acquisitions', pl. xxii)

near the eastern edge of the stone that covered the arm-ring, the portion of which was removed and brought to the National Museum of Ireland for safekeeping. The original surface of the stone had been removed by some broad implement, leaving a series of grooves on the exterior. Ó Ríordáin argued that the significance of the markings was indiscernible and did not fit in with any known forms of inscription. He believed that some markings were, however, too complex to represent the marks of tool sharpening. It may be that they were intended as marks relating to the hiding-place of the silver hoard and that they held significance for the person who inscribed them.[29]

The Carrowmore arm-rings (fig. 4) were of a class of Viking arm-ring well represented in Irish collections. Two were ornamented and the third was plain.[30] All three were discoloured to an unusual depth and analysis showed that chlorine was present in the soil, which, acting over a period of a thousand years, could cause chemical action like that on the arm-rings.[31] Similar arm-rings have been dated by associated finds in Britain (such as in the Cuerdale hoard) to the early tenth century. Ó Ríordáin posited that, 'in the absence of data to the contrary', one can 'take it that the same dating holds for the Irish

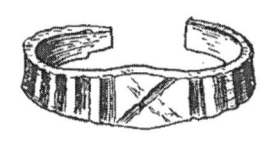

4. Carrowmore silver hoard, showing the three ornamented arm-rings
(source: Ó Ríordáin, 'Recent acquisitions', p. 176)

bracelets and place them also, in the main, in the tenth century' and c.911 has been suggested as the deposition date.[32] It has been proposed that these arm-rings show an Eastern influence that travelled up the Russian trade route, then, because of the Vikings, from the Black Sea to the Baltic and then onwards to Britain and Ireland.[33] A contrary theory posed by Bøe is that these arm-rings were a 'Norse-Irish speciality':

> St Andrews cross in the enlarged portion and transversal grooves on the end produced with a stamp or punch is somewhat of a Norse-Irish speciality. At all events it is much more common on Viking silver in Ireland than in Norway. Personally, I am inclined to the opinion that it was introduced from Arabian Spain to Ireland and from there to Norway.[34]

Ó Ríordáin believed that Bøe's suggestion of influence from Arabian Spain was worth considering, and certain arguments may be advanced in support of it. In favour of this theory is the fact that a Viking raid on Spain occurred c.859 and some of the Viking ships, having taken part in the attacks on the western coast of the peninsula and on the Mediterranean coast of Morocco, returned northwards to Ireland, bringing Moorish prisoners with them.[35] Also, considering that the silver arm-rings found in Scandinavia are more advanced in design than those found in Ireland, it is possible that they date to a later period.

In the case of the Carrowmore arm-rings, it is significant that in the same townland there are the remains of a disused silver mine. This mine was noted as having been worked in the late eighteenth century and it was also re-used between 1908 and 1910.[36] While there is no indication that the mine had been used prior to the eighteenth century, it is potentially significant that a silver supply should be available in the wider area of the discovery location of silver arm-rings and, according to Ó Ríordáin, 'one of which, because of its unornamented surface, leads one to believe that the objects were, in all probability, made on the spot'.[37] A list of ancient silver mines, when plotted on a map with the find-locations of Viking silver artefacts, shows a 'remarkable coincidence of distribution' that suggests 'Viking silver ornaments of Irish provenance were made in Ireland and that the material is the product of silver mines in this country'.[38] One potential issue with this, however, is that the distribution pattern of the ornaments may have been impacted by Viking raiding and trading.[39]

During the early tenth century (the likely deposition date for the arm-rings), Norse influence in Ireland had weakened, and the period of intensive Viking activity commencing $c.914$ had not yet begun. Thus, the creation and distribution of the arm-rings may have occurred pre-914. The Carrowmore arm-rings are outside the area of the ancient mines, but the very existence of the modern mine could suggest a source for this silver. Additionally, folklore tells of the now-archaic custom of holding a fair in the area of Carrowmore.[40] If a fair at Carrowmore existed in the ninth century, the arm-rings may have been crafted and/or traded in this context. Further indication that Carrowmore was a significant ancient and early medieval site is clear from archaeological evidence. Ó Ríordáin noted that three axes were found in the area of Carrowmore/Glentogher. These artefacts suggest that Carrowmore was once a site of ancient significance. This importance may have carried through to the early medieval period, when an ecclesiastical complex was erected there in the sixth century.[41] The medieval church site at Carrowmore and the neighbouring complexes of Clonca and Culdaff may have attracted Scandinavian raiders in the earliest phases of Viking expansion to Ireland, as there are substantial annalistic references to raids on monastic sites throughout the country. This is explored further in Chapter 2.

ROOSKY, CLONMANY

In the townland of Roosky, Clonmany, situated in east Inishowen, four silver arm-rings were discovered in the wall of a cashel in 1966 (fig. 5). The monument was known locally as 'The Pound' and was situated on the left bank of the Clonmany River. The wall

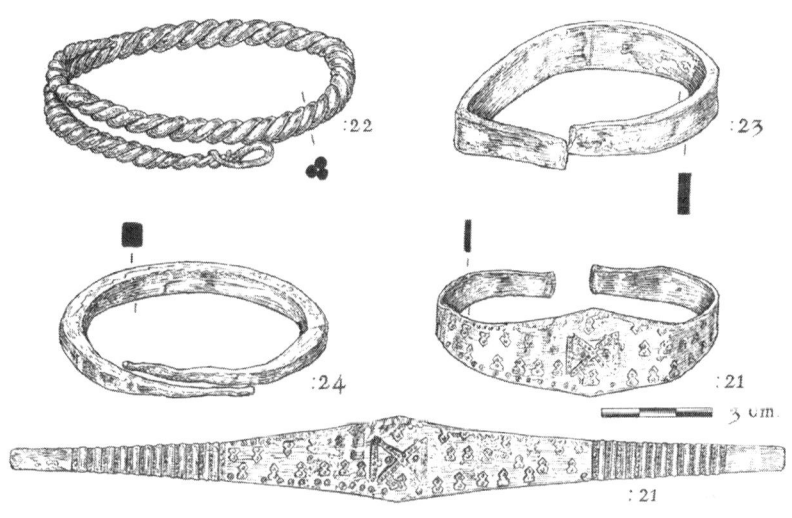

5. Viking silver hoard of four arm-rings found at Roosky, Clonmany
(source: Raftery, 'A hoard of Viking silver bracelets', p. 134)

of the monument was built of stones that did not appear to have been laid regularly but were likely heaped to form a rubble wall. While demolishing the wall of the fort, four silver arm-rings were discovered by the landowner in such circumstances that it appeared they had fallen down with the wall itself.[42] The circumstances of the find parallels the case of the Viking silver hoard that was discovered in a similar monument at Carraig Aille, Lough Gur, Co. Limerick, in which the hoard was hidden in the interstices between the stones of the wall.[43]

The potential date range for the Roosky hoard is from c.900 to the early eleventh century. Joseph Raftery rebuked Ó Ríordáin's efforts to cite Muslim Spain as a potential source for this bracelet type, and instead suggested that they were originally a Scandinavian import:

> In all the circumstances it is hard to escape the conclusion that bracelets of the type under discussion must be Scandinavian and probably Norse. In shape, they have no forerunners in Ireland and the nature of the ornamentation on them has no parallels amongst native Irish material. Ireland, then, would not appear to have much claim to being the country of their origin, though some personal ornaments of this kind may have been made here by Norse or, indeed, Irish silversmiths.[44]

Following this point, Raftery objected to Ó Ríordáin's theory that Viking silver objects found in Ireland were likely made here, in conjunction with ancient silver mines, arguing that manufacture of this kind was limited in Ireland.[45] Raftery cited Dolley regarding the find location of the Roosky hoard, only a short distance from the coastline. The majority of Viking hoards in Ireland were found within a day's march of the Irish coast.[46] As we have discussed, the Vikings in Ireland dominated coastal areas and sea inlets.

LURGABRACK, DUNFANAGHY

The most recent discovery of a Viking silver hoard in Donegal occurred in September 2011. A hoard of silver arm-rings was found through illegal and unlicensed metal detecting at a souterrain in Lurgabrack, on the Horn Head Peninsula, in the north of the county. The souterrain was situated in an area of sand dunes, just north-west of Tramore Strand. The arm-rings were discovered on the ground of the souterrain.[47] The souterrain had drystone walls and the roof was composed of large flagstones. The hoard apparently hidden in sandy soil, just south of a pair of projecting jambs and lintels.[48] The arm-rings appeared to have been placed close together on the ground.

The disposition of the objects within the souterrain is significant. As we have already seen, the Raphoe silver hoard was found at the base of a drystone ditch, while the Roosky hoard was found in the wall of a cashel. Similarly, the Lurgabrack hoard was likely hidden in the souterrain for safety or concealment.[49] This could indicate that the artefacts had fallen into Irish hands as they were hidden in native Irish settlement types.[50] The circumstances of the Viking artefacts ending up in Irish possession (gift exchange, plunder, ransom and tribute among others) and the socio-economic relationship between the native people and the Vikings is considered further in Chapter 2. A number of other monuments are recorded around the find-spot at Largatreany, Claggan, Pollaguill, Muntermellan, Corgannive Glebe and Murroe (where a silver ingot was found) including a hut site, enclosure and field system in Lurgabrack.[51] Meanwhile, in the neighbouring townland of Cloghernagh, there is a hilltop cashel. Maeve Sikora argues that 'these monuments broadly indicate settlement in the area during the period in which the hoard was probably deposited' as 'stray finds of archaeological artefacts dating broadly to the early medieval period are also recorded from the sandhills'.[52]

All eight of the silver arm-rings from the Lurgabrack hoard are of the plain ring-money type. Ring-money is relatively rare in Ireland, occurring in complete form in four hoards and as a handful of single finds, the majority of which have no recorded context.[53] The term 'ring-money' has been used to describe plain penannular rings formed from a single rod of metal. The theory is that the plainness of the rings indicates their use as a form of currency, rather than as a piece of jewellery. Sikora explains that this theory is supported 'by the fact that some seem to have been manufactured to a target weight of $c.24.0 \pm 0.8$gm'.[54] Ring-money appears to have originated in the Irish Sea region and is represented in approximately one-third of all known Scottish Viking-Age hoards, from which over ninety complete examples and a few hundred fragments of ring-money are known. These artefacts generally date to between the mid-tenth and the mid-eleventh centuries (through coin-dating), and the Skaill hoard, with a deposition date of $c.950$ to 970, is the earliest coin-dated hoard to contain ring-money in Scotland.[55] Examples of ring-money have been found both lozenge-sectioned and round-sectioned, although this does not seem to hold any chronological importance. Differences in the ornamentation of these rings may be chronologically significant, and Sikora cites Graham-Campbell's suggestion that ring-money with flattened terminals are later than unflattened examples, at least in Scotland.[56]

Four of the Lurgabrack arm-rings have round sections and four have lozenge-shaped sections (fig. 6). Of the round-sectioned examples, three have plain and one has flattened terminals. Of the rings with lozenge-shaped sections, three have flattened terminals and only one has plain terminals.[57] The presence of three rings with terminals of spatulate form indicate that the hoard dates from the 970s or later.[58] The silver of the arm-rings derives from a number of sources that circulated around the Irish Sea region at this time.[59] The Lurgabrack hoard is the largest find of ring-money in Ireland.

The Lurgabrack hoard is a recent addition to the large number of previously known Viking-Age hoards in the county, joining the Burt, 'North-West Inishowen', Raphoe, Carrowmore and Roosky

6. Eight examples of Viking silver ring-money from Lurgabrack
(source: Sikora, 'A hoard of Viking-Age silver ring-money from Lurgabrack', p. 191)

hoards. The Raphoe hoard also contained ring-money associated with Hiberno-Scandinavian rings, although this is considered by Graham-Campbell to be a prototype rather than true Scotto-Scandinavian ring-money.[60] The Lurgabrack hoard is likely to have been deposited between the mid-tenth and the mid-eleventh century, corresponding with dated hoards of ring-money found in Ireland and Scotland. That this hoard of Scottish-Scandinavian type ring-money should be found in Co. Donegal is

> not altogether surprising given the geographical proximity of this part of Ireland to Scotland. The fact that the location is

coastal is also interesting and suggests that the hoard, exclusively of Scottish-type material, had recently come into Irish hands as a result of contact with Scandinavian Scotland.[61]

RINNARAW, PORTNABLAGH

It has been suggested that the remains of a house at Rinnaraw cashel can be compared with similar buildings excavated at Viking sites in the Scottish Western Isles. The foundations of a rectangular stone-built house were identified on the north-west sector of the site. The site at Rinnaraw, Portnablagh, in north Donegal is situated on the western side of Sheephaven Bay, an area of large peninsulas and fjord-like sea loughs. The deep deposits of boulder clay in the area are suitable for agriculture, as reflected in the concentration of archaeological monuments (earthen ringforts, stone cashels, promontory forts, crannogs and isolated souterrains) in this area. The site was classified as a cashel in Brian Lacey's *Archaeological survey* of the county, based on an arc of large stones located along the edge of a sub-circular stone platform.[62] The term 'cashel' suggests a circular stone enclosure with more structures in the interior. This description, however, does not adequately describe the site at Rinnaraw. Before excavation, all that was visible was the stone arc and the foundations of an oval structure within.[63]

The majority of the sites in the immediate vicinity of Rinnaraw are stone enclosures, some with traces of internal structures and several in a poor state of preservation, much like Rinnaraw itself, where the enclosing cashel wall had been almost completely destroyed. The majority of settlement was on the coast and comprised promontory forts and stone cashels, which were often stronger and more defensive than other forms of settlement. Michelle Comber suspects that 'this might reflect a need to defend the coast, or at least keep a tight grip on it. Perhaps some of the cashels and promontory forts served as military posts or watch-posts'.[64] Six monuments are situated within 2km of the site. The closest is a crannog in Woodhill, on Loch an tSeisigh. The other five sites are cashels at Faugher, Breaghy, Dunrudian Hill, Cashelnagalliagh and Portnablagh.[65] Marine resources likely had a significant role in the economy of these coastal sites, though whether

7. Potential Viking-influenced medieval house at Rinnaraw
(source: Comber et al., 'Tom Fanning's excavations at Rinnaraw', p. 108)

their primary function was seafood exploitation or the control of communications or defence (later, perhaps, from Viking invaders) is unknown.[66]

In 1988, the form of the house at Rinnaraw was revealed through excavation, being rectangular in plan and of drystone construction. The corners of the structure were rounded externally and right-angled internally.[67] Structural features were uncovered in the interior that resulted in its classification as a domestic house. The most extensive internal feature was a paved section of flooring that may indicate a separate paved 'room'. The remains of a hearth with charcoal and burnt clay were uncovered just north of the centre of the house. The remains of two middens were discovered, one of which featured winkles, cockles and barnacles, along with bone and iron slag fragments and some small finds including a pot sherd, two bone points, a small iron handle, an iron knife fragment and a tuyère on the lower levels. Due to the complex structure of the midden in the north of the house, Comber speculated that it was multi-period.[68] Between the house and enclosure wall, evidence of human activity was uncovered in the south-eastern corner where the remains of a 'fire-pit' were found. Other finds included some quern fragments, whetstones, a saddle quern and a broken trough quern, which may indicate a link between the site and Scottish sites of a similar nature.[69]

The lower levels, under the walls of the house, date to the late eighth or early ninth century and are associated with the building of the house. Radio-carbon testing indicates that the house walls were built later in the ninth century. Molluscs dated from the midden infer that the upper levels accumulated a century or two later, suggesting that the site was in use for two or three hundred years.[70] The house at Rinnaraw (fig. 7) is structurally similar to two Irish examples, the Phase 3 house (late ninth to tenth century) at Rathmullan, Co. Down, and House B at Leacanabuaile, Co. Kerry, but the most striking similarity comes from further afield, off the Scottish coast.[71] Some of the Norse structures excavated on the Orkneys had similar dimensions to Rinnaraw, with externally rounded corners. The main phase of activity at Rinnaraw dates to the ninth century, the same period that saw increasing levels of Viking activity in the Donegal area. Comber believed that 'the occupants at Rinnaraw may have had some contact with, or knowledge of, the Vikings (probably from Scotland), though what form this may have taken is uncertain'.[72]

MISCELLANEOUS

There are a number of possible Viking finds and sites in Donegal that are worth mentioning. Graham-Campbell mentioned a possible Viking-Age ingot hoard found in 1848 while demolishing the fort of Liss, at Corr, a coastal site in western Donegal. The Liss hoard consisted of seven silver 'lumps' that were later sold to a pedlar. They are described as having been square and plain, like large dice, however Viking silver ingots are usually oblong.[73] Graham-Campbell also cited the unpublished fragment of an ingot found at Murroe, in Clondahorky.[74] A hoard of over one hundred amber beads was found in the townland of Meenalabban during turf-cutting in the spring of 1932. No associated objects were found and, therefore, there was no data on which to date the find.[75] At Garrygort, George Henry Kinahan noted 'two rude ancient structures of squarish slabs of stone set on edge'. They were known locally as 'Dane's houses'.[76] Contemporary searches at the location indicated by Kinahan and in the surrounding area failed to reveal any trace of the structures.[77]

Lacey's *Archaeological survey of County Donegal* referred to a Viking ringed-pin that was found on the shores of Kinnegar beach, and cited Richard Warner, who inspected the site and indicated it may have been a storm-disturbed Viking burial.[78] Further contact with Warner revealed similarities between the Kinnegar ringed-pin and one found at the Larne Viking grave that likely dates to the late ninth or early tenth century. A group of workmen constructing a railway discovered a burial in the sand containing a male skeleton with associated grave finds of the Viking period. The Larne ringed-pin was described as follows:

> Pin and ring have a fine dark-green patina which is corroded in places. The upper shank is oval in cross-section to just below mid-point where it splays slightly and assumes a flat rectangular section as it tapers to the point which is damaged. It is decorated with a series of four transverse grooves just below the head. The head is of the looped-over variety and has a sweated closure.[79]

Ringed-pins are common in Viking graves. The simple form of the Larne example does not allow for close dating, but its frequent occurrence in Viking Scotland and Scandinavia suggests a date in the late ninth or early tenth century. We can assume that the Kinnegar ringed-pin is of a similar style and date to the Larne ringed-pin, given Warner's recommendation. Ó Ríordáin also notes a bronze brooch found at Grousehall, Tievebane, another found in the sand-dunes of Inishbofin and a broken bronze ringed-pin that was likely found at a coastal site at the Rosses.[80]

Tomás Ó Canann has suggested that the probable inauguration site of the Ua Canannáin dynasty at Carraig an Dúnain (Doonan Rock), on the summit of Doonan Hill, had a possible Viking origin. This mound-like landform, just west of Donegal town, is now largely destroyed. Ó Cannan argued that, although cruder in form,

Archaeological evidence for Vikings in Co. Donegal

and possibly larger, Doonan Rock resonates with the Viking *ping* 'assembly' mound, at Tynwald Hill, on the Isle of Man. The Tynwald site 'is now understood by archaeologists to be representative of Viking ceremonial mounds throughout the entire Norse Irish Sea province'.[81] Ó Cannan also states, however, that the 'absence of an obvious stepped profile in the Ordnance Survey sketch of Doonan Rock, a characteristic feature found at such Viking sites as Tynwald, Govan and Thingmote (College Green, Dublin), raises a cautionary flag'.[82] The mound at Doonan Rock could represent the first archaeological confirmation of a possible Norse settlement (*longphort*) at the foot of the River Eske, but there is not sufficient evidence to prove this theory.[83] Considering the proximity of this archaeological site to Donegal Town, or *Baile Dún na nGall*, this could further corroborate the possible Viking origin of the name 'Fort of the Foreigners'.

* * *

To conclude, the presence of both Hiberno-Norse and plain arm-rings in the Raphoe, Carrowmore, Roosky and 'North-West Inishowen' hoards suggests that all four are of a similar date, *c.*850 to 950.[84] The Anglo-Saxon coin hoard from Burt and the Lurgabrack ring-money hoard are the only identifiable post-950 examples. Lurgabrack is located a few kilometres west of the medieval house at Rinnaraw, which parallels Viking houses of the Scottish Isles. This possibly indicates the movement of Vikings from the north-east of the county, around the Inishowen Peninsula, to the north-west of the county. The likely conclusion drawn from the archaeological evidence for Vikings in Co. Donegal is that it does not represent wealthy, successful Norse settlers, but rather derives from the short-lived and unsuccessful presence of Viking raiders, hence the association of some hoards with Irish settlements. This is investigated further in the next chapter, through documentary evidence.

2. Documentary evidence for Vikings in Co. Donegal

Ireland suffered no foreign conquest until the eighth century.[1] Society on the eve of the arrival of the Vikings consisted of a number of large political kingdoms, or dynasties, and many smaller petty kingdoms within larger power structures. Ireland was wealthy in terms of people, animals and agricultural production, thus making it an attractive place for plunder and, later, colonization. Wealth was concentrated in key areas, particularly the residences of kings and lords, but most of all at monastic sites.[2] Ireland changed significantly during the Viking Age. Despite the widespread perturbation caused by the Vikings, they made no major territorial gains in Ireland, with only one or two examples of petty kingdoms disappearing as a result of Viking raids. Vikings established towns along the coast, which introduced changes to Irish society and the economy.[3]

The popular perception of Vikings as merciless warriors who terrorized the Irish landscape was partly the result of propaganda, and intentional obscuring by the learned classes who wrote the annals.[4] This chapter focuses on references to Vikings in Donegal in the annals. The Viking presence in Donegal, and in Ireland more broadly, and the construction of the sources we now rely on, are also considered. It is important to understand the Vikings not just as 'ruthless raiders', but also as people who fought vicious political wars against the native polity and, at other times, allied with Irish chieftans and subsequently became assimilated in their culture.

VIKINGS IN IRELAND: AN OVERVIEW

Substantial parts of Scotland, particularly the Northern and Western Isles, were conquered by Vikings in the early ninth century. Viking settlement in Scotland corresponds chronologically to what

Donnchadh Ó Corráin referred to as the 'prelude to the Viking wars' in Ireland, the first phase of which occurs from 795 to c.830.[5] Thus, while some of the raids on Ireland came directly from Scandinavia, some also came from Scottish Viking settlements. Accordingly, the first recorded attack in 795, on *Rechru* or *Rechrainn*, is more likely to have been on Rathlin Island than on Lambay. Lacey has suggested that Rathlin O'Birne, an island off the coast of Co. Donegal, is *Rechru*.[6] The Vikings made their way around the north-west coastline, and Inishmurray and Inishbofin were plundered next.[7] In 821 Howth was plundered, in 824 Skellig Michael was raided and during the 830s Glendalough and Clondalkin were subject to attack. The monastery of Derry, *Dubh Regles* (Black Church), had been destroyed in 788, but the Vikings were 'routed' at Derry in 833.[8] Church sites were targeted as areas of great wealth. This first phase of Viking raiding was a part-time summer endeavour, after which they returned to the Scandinavian (or Scottish) homelands.

The second phase of Viking activity in Ireland was an overwintering period of Viking penetration and Irish reaction that took place from c.835 to 902. This phase of Viking activity differed from the hit-and-run attacks that characterized the first phase. Viking raiders penetrated Irish coastal areas and traversed boldly on inland rivers and lakes, with increased intensity and fervour. Large fleets began overwintering in the mid-830s at Dublin, Annagassan, Cork, Lough Ree, Dunrally and Waterford. Some of these *longphorts* (overwintering sites) became permanent settlement camps. In 839 a Viking fleet was based on Lough Neagh, 'whence they ravaged the lands of the Northern Uí Néill, Airgialla and Ulaid'.[9] In 852, Óláfr set up the kingdom of Dublin, a major event in Viking-Age Ireland. From 876 to 916, *Cogadh Gaedhel re Gallaibh* reports 'forty years rest' from Viking activity, and although this has been disputed, a 'Dublin hiatus' did take place from 902 to 917 during which time the Dublin Viking leadership was driven out.[10]

Phase three occurred from 917 until 937 when permanent settlement took place. After this phase, it became increasingly difficult to denote specific Viking activity, as their actions were intimately interwoven with that of the native Irish.[11] Historians generally concur that the Viking Age ended during the eleventh century, considering the Norman Conquest of England in 1066 as one of the last great battles in the Viking wars. In an Irish context, the Battle of Tara in 980 has been proposed as a suitable point of transition from the 'Viking' period to the 'Hiberno-Norse' period.[12] Between 980 and 1014, when the Battle of Clontarf took place, 'Viking' Dublin had become a true Hiberno-Norse trade port.[13] This chapter considers the evidence for Vikings in Donegal from the beginning of the Viking Age until the end of the Hiberno-Norse period.

SOURCES FOR VIKING SETTLEMENT IN IRELAND

It is difficult to establish when and where Vikings may have founded their settlement camps in Ireland. Most historians would agree that the annals are often ambiguous in their description of Viking camps, as this was not their priority when composing the written record.[14] Emer Purcell has considered the issues surrounding their origins and chronology.[15] The annals focus on propagandizing the 'brutal Viking warrior' by emphasizing, first, their raids on church settlements and, secondly, their political campaigns against the native Irish, either alone or in alliance with other native kingdoms.

It is important to be aware that the similarity of different annals is due to the fact that a common source, the Chronicle of Ireland, influenced most of these accounts. Annalists also copied from other annals, such as those who compiled the Annals of the Four Masters. These were created in the 1630s, mostly extracting information from the Annals of Ulster, but it was also closely related to the Fragmentary Annals of Ireland.[16] Pseudo-historical narratives in the Fragmentary Annals of Ireland were developed in the eleventh and twelfth centuries to celebrate the victories of native Irish kings over Viking marauders. Furthermore, the author of *Cogadh Gaedhel re Gallaibh* interpreted and re-wrote stories with some degree of creative licence and, as such, historical accuracy was given second place to propaganda.[17] Native kingships sought to highlight the prestige of their ancestors who overcame foreign enemies, predominantly as a result of the growing sense of Irish identity in the face of a foreign 'other'.[18] The Irish annals, while providing very little detail about the nature and form of Viking settlement in Ireland, can give an indication as to when they were most active, and where.[19] The Annals of Ulster are considered most reliable and, as such, will be the focus of this text.

Clare Downham considered the possible reason for the lack of definitive evidence for Viking settlement during the ninth century, arguing that some camps

> may have been as fleeting as a sheltered stretch of water where ships moored overnight, or an army making use of an abandoned ringfort to rest and recoup before pushing on towards a more distant goal. Such settlements might be invisible in the archaeological record and may not have seemed significant enough to warrant report in Irish chronicles.[20]

It is equally hard to determine if the presence of a Viking fleet in a particular area, as recounted by the annals, was synonymous with Viking settlement. Some camps can be identified from references by the use of settlement terminology, such as the word *longphort*, translated as 'ship port'. Settlements at Linn Duachaill (Annagassan) and Dublin were characterized by this term but later it referred not only to Viking settlements. One example of a *longphort* relating to Gaelic settlement is a fifteenth-century reference to Cenn Maghair (Kinnaweer) in Donegal.[21] At times, Viking settlement camps can be presumed where Vikings were reported to have stayed at a particular location for a prolonged period, or because a group of Vikings were identifiable by their connection to a particular site.[22]

DONEGAL AND SCOTLAND: A CLOSE CONNECTION

As previously mentioned, it is believed that most of the Vikings who first plundered Ireland's shores came from the Scottish Isles. Ó Corráin argued that *Laithlinn/Lochlainn* may have been Viking Scotland, although the term was used to denote Norway from the eleventh century onwards. Some historians, such as Mary Valante and Colmán Etchingham, have opined that *Laithlinn* in every period more likely represented Norway or a region within Norway.[23]

This coincides with the theory that the Vikings who arrived on Irish shores came predominantly from Scotland.[24] It is true to say that Donegal, in particular, had a strong link with Scotland throughout the early medieval period prior to the arrival of the Vikings. Lacey's analysis of the Colum Cille Cross at Ray Church, Falcarragh, supports this. St Colum Cille (also known as St Columba), born c.521 into the Cenél Conaill dynasty, was credited with spreading Christianity to Scotland and founding large numbers of religious institutions there, including at Iona. St John's cross at Iona was probably later copied at Ray.[25] In 793 Vikings attacked Lindisfarne. The following year they plundered the Hebrides. Vikings attacked Iona in 795 and 802 and in 806 they killed sixty-eight monks at Martyr's Bay.[26] Viking raiders thus went from Iona to Rathlin Island, or possibly Rathlin O'Birne Island, in 795.

ASSAROE, BALLYSHANNON

In 837 a group of Vikings were slaughtered at Assaroe by the Cenél Conaill: 'at Eas-Ruaidh, now Assaroe, near Ballyshannon, county of Donegal, they (heathens) were defeated by the Cinel-Conaill, the descendents of Conall Gulban [...]'.[27] The source of this information, *Cogadh Gaedhel re Gallaibh*, is not as reliable as the Annals of Ulster. *Cogadh Gaedhel re Gallaibh* may be subject to exaggeration, inaccuracy and bias. References in other annals, however, lend support to this account. The Annals of Ulster state that Vikings were active in 837 on Lough Erne, from which the River Erne flows north into the Atlantic, at the southern end of Donegal: 'the churches of all Loch Éirne, including Cluain Eóis and Daiminis, were destroyed by the heathens'.[28] A medieval church site was located at Assaroe. The first phase of plundering church raids (795 to c.830) was reaching its end, but Vikings were still targeting sites of monastic wealth. Assaroe Falls, a waterfall near the medieval church site, was situated on the River Erne. It is plausible that the Vikings active on Lough Erne made their way up the River Erne into southern Donegal to plunder Assaroe, or vice versa, where they were defeated by the Cenél Conaill.

LINN SAILEACH – LOUGH SWILLY?

The Annals of Ulster refer to Vikings on Linn Saileach in 842: 'a naval force of the Norsemen was on the Bóinn at Linn Rois. There was *also* a naval force of the Norsemen at Linn Sailech in Ulaid'.[29] The Annals of the Four Masters has a similar entry in 841, although it also indicates a fleet of Vikings at Linn Duachaill in the same reference: 'a fleet of Norsemen on the Boinn, at Linn Rois. Another fleet of them at Linn Saileach, in Ulster. Another fleet of them at Linn Duachaill'.[30] The same year, the Annals of Ulster mention 'Linn' again: 'Mórán son of Indrechtach, abbot of Clochar Mac nDaiméni, was taken prisoner by the foreigners of Linn, and later died on their hands'.[31] Downham considers that a *longphort* may have existed at Lough Swilly: 'a camp may have existed at Lough Swilly in Co. Donegal. A fleet is mentioned there [...] alongside references to fleets at Rosnaree and Lough Foyle. While it can be argued that bases existed at Rosnaree and Lough Foyle, the case for Lough Swilly is only made by association'.[32] Lacey, however, argues that Ulaid, translated in the Annals of the Four Masters as 'Ulster', in this context more likely refers to Co. Down; therefore, the Linn Saileach is not Lough Swilly.[33]

According to Siobhan McDermott, Linn Sailech was on the coastline of Dál Fiatach, the territory in the north-east of Ireland.[34] Thomas McErlean has also suggested that Linn Sailech was somewhere on the coastline of Dál Fiatach.[35] Lenore Fischer proposed, however, that the site should be identified as Lough Swilly, Co. Donegal.[36] P.J. Bracken, in agreement with Downham and Fischer, argued that there is 'no place-name or historical evidence' to support the identification of this place 'anywhere in the province-kingdom of Ulaid'.[37] Bracken stated that 'apart from the identification of Linn Sailech as being "in Ulaid" in the Annals of Ulster there is no reason to support any suggestion'.[38] He wrote that Linn Sailech is Lough Swilly, or 'the sea inlet lying between the western side of the Inishowen Peninsula and the Fanad Peninsula, in Co. Donegal, in the province-kingdom of Northern Uí Néill'.[39]

While no definite evidence exists for settlement on Lough Swilly, one must consider the geographical and archaeological evidence. Lough Swilly is a glacial fjord lying between the Inishowen Peninsula and the Fanad Peninsula. Most of the archaeological evidence discussed in Chapter 1 was found in Inishowen, although dating to a century later. Kinnegar beach, the possible site of a Viking burial where a bronze ringed-pin was discovered, is situated on the western shore of Lough Swilly. Moreover, Viking mortuary rituals were symbolically enacted on the shore because the Vikings'

> lived experience was dominated by the interplay of sea and land [...] symbolizing the passage between life and death, this world, and the next. The Vikings, like other coastal societies, were a sea-orientated people for whom water represented a route way rather than a boundary.[40]

Lough Swilly is one of only three glacial fjords in Ireland, alongside Carlingford Lough and Killary Harbour. Vikings, whose very epithet comes from the work *vík*, meaning fjord, were particularly familiar with navigating this type of sea inlet. Despite this, due to lack of evidence, the Viking connection with Lough Swilly must remain hypothetical.

MAGH ITHA

The Annals of Ulster reference the defeat of Vikings at Magh Itha in 845: 'Niall son of Áed inflicted a battle-rout on the heathens in Mag Ítha'.[41] The exact location of the territory of Magh Itha is subject to speculation. Lacey considers it to be in east Donegal, in the lower valley of the River Finn, immediately north of Barnesmore Gap.[42] John O'Donovan places Magh Itha along the Finn, near Lough Swilly. Ó Corráin describes Magh Itha as the 'valuable plain south of Greenan Mountain'.[43] After the Battle of Clóiteach in 789, this territory changed hands from the Cenél Conaill to the Cenél nEogain.[44] Although the exact location of the site within Co. Donegal is disputed, it was the location of a battle between the Cenél nEogain and the Vikings. Magh Itha was an important territory in prehistoric and medieval times, renowned in Irish mythology as the site of the first battle fought in Ireland.

DONEGAL KINGS AND THE GALL-GHAEDHIL

During the 850s, the Gall-Ghaedhil emerged in the documentary record for a short period. This band of Vikings likely originated in

Scotland as a generation of mixed Scottish/Irish/Viking descent that broke away from the larger Viking dynasties.[45] The earliest references to the Gall-Ghaedhil in 856 indicate an immediate connection to Donegal, perhaps due to its proximity to Scotland, as Áed Findliath, king of Aileach, engages them in battle:

> Áed, king of Ailech, the king of greatest prowess in his time, gave battle to the fleet of the Gall-Gaedil (that is, they are Irish, and foster-children of the Norse, and sometimes they are even called Norsemen). Áed defeated them, and slaughtered the Gall-Gaedil, and Áed brought many heads away with him.[46]

In the Annals of Ulster, the Gall-Ghaedhil allied with Mael Sechnaill, king of Tara, against the leaders of the Viking dynasties, Ímar and Amlaíb, kings of Dublin: 'great warfare between the Vikings and Mael Sechnaill, who was supported by the Gall-Goídil'.[47] The same year, they were in the north, where Áed Findliath defeated them at *Glenn Foichle* (Glenelly, in the barony of Strabane, on the now Donegal/Tyrone border): 'Áed son of Niall inflicted a great rout on the Norse-Irish in Glenn Foichle and a vast number of them were slaughtered by him'.[48] The Gall-Ghaedhil later allied with the Cenél Fiachach of the Southern Uí Néill but were defeated by Dublin Vikings and the king of Osraige.[49] Following this, the Gall-Ghaedhil disappear from the historical record for some time.

DONEGAL KINGS AND DUBLIN VIKINGS

By the 860s, Áed Findliath, king of Aileach, had fostered an alliance with Óláfr, king of the Dublin Vikings, when his daughter was wedded to Óláfr. The aim of this alliance was to oppose Mael Sechnaill. In 861 and 862, they took on Mael Sechnaill and the Southern Uí Néill.[50] In 866, however, the alliance crumbled as Óláfr left Ireland. The same year, Áed destroyed the Vikings' *longphort* along the north coast and defeated them in battle at Lough Foyle:

> A complete muster of the North was gathered by Áed Finnliath, and he raided the bases of the foreigners, wherever they were in Fochla, both in Cenél nEógain and Dál nAraide; and he brought

away their herds, and their garments, and their booty, and their many possessions.[51]

The entry in the Annals of Ulster described how 'Aed son of Niall plundered the *longphuirt* of the foreigners; i.e., in the territory of the north, both in Cenél nEógain and Dál nAiridi and took away their heads, their flocks and their herds from camp by battle. A victory was gained over them at Loch Febail and twelve score heads taken thereby'.[52] This entry is very interesting because, through its mention of 'their flocks and herds', it specifies the concept of the *longphort* as a settlement with a hinterland and associated agricultural interests. The existence of supporting settlements around these *longphort* sites indicates that these examples were well-established bases.[53] Coastal camps in the north may have been a springboard for Óláfr's campaigns in Scotland or Áed might have encouraged Óláfr's men to establish bases in the northern part of Ulster to strengthen the control of the Cenél nEógain.[54]

Following the death of Máel Sechnaill in 862, the high-kingship passed to Áed Findliath. It seems that he may no longer have needed Scandinavian support and that this resulted in his destruction of their northern *longphorts* in 866. Purcell and Sheehan proposed that the Vikings had 'served their purpose for him while he was king-in-waiting, but by 866 he had no further need of them'.[55] Stephen Harrison argued that this was a 'pivotal' event, 'effectively preventing the development of any Norse towns in the area' and was 'blamed for the later decline of the Uí Néill, who subsequently lacked access to the resources that flowed from sites such as Dublin, Waterford and Limerick'.[56] This on-again/off-again alliance, however, had a complex historical record. In 871 the Annals of Ulster described a joint attack on Dunseverick Castle, Co. Antrim, by the Vikings and Cenél nEógain: 'the storming of Dún Sobairche, which had never been achieved before: the foreigners were at it with the Cenél Eógain'.[57]

In relation to Donegal, the problem with the 866 entry in the Annals of Ulster is that it does not indicate where precisely these *longphort* settlements were. There are three known settlements in the northern territory: Strangford Lough, Lough Neagh and Lough Foyle. It has also been posited that there was an encampment at Lough Swilly.[58] It is interesting to note that the reference outlines territories in *both* 'Cenél nEógain and Dál Araidi', which would at least indicate Lough Foyle, with the possibility of other settlements in the Cenél nEógain region.

LOUGH FOYLE

As mentioned in the last section, the Annals of Ulster provide information about a major battle that took place at Lough Foyle during this Donegal-led military campaign against Vikings in the territory of the Northern Uí Néill in 866: 'a victory was gained over them at Loch Febail and twelve score heads taken thereby'.[59] Mentions of Vikings 'at' Lough Foyle can be found throughout the ninth and tenth century. At the end of the ninth century, despite earlier attempts by Áed Findliath to decimate them, the Vikings were still in action: 'Armagh was raided by the foreigners of Lough Foyle, and Cumascach was taken by them, and his son, Áed son of Cumascach, was killed'.[60] Downham believes that Vikings being described as 'of' somewhere implies settlement: 'I would argue that where Vikings 'of' a particular place are found mentioned in chronicles of the ninth century, there is a strong possibility that a camp was established at these sites'.[61] It is plausible, given the references, that there were Viking settlements in the Co. Derry/Lough Foyle area.

CARRICKABRAGHY, ISLE OF DOAGH

Further documentary evidence of Vikings in Co. Donegal can be found in a bardic poem called *Ard na scéla, a mheic na ccuach*, which translates as 'High the tidings, O son of the goblets'.[62] The poem, which was ascribed to the famous bard Flann Mac Lonáin, was written as a eulogy to Éichnechán, lord of Fanad, who died in 906, according to the Annals of Ulster. The poem survives only in much later manuscripts. The date and author of the poem have been the subjects of much debate. According to the Annals of Ulster, Mac Lonáin died in 891, or in 896, both of which would preclude his authorship of an elegy for a chief who died in 906.[63] The Annals of the Four Masters put his death at 916, which means he could be the author of the poem. Ó Corráin argues that the poem was 'impossibly fathered' on Flann Mac Lónain and suggests a more likely date of composition in the eleventh or twelfth century.[64] Lacey argues that 'there is very little reason for doubting that Éichnechán was the real subject of the poem and that it was composed at some time shortly after his death'.[65] In any case, Éichnechán died in the early tenth century: 'Eigneachan, son of Dalach, son of Muircheartach, lord of Cinel Conaill, died'.[66] Thus, the information provided in the poem likely pertains to the mid- to late ninth century.

The author describes how Éichnechán had been compelled to marry his three daughters Duibhlinn, Bé Binn and Bé Buadha to three Viking leaders to prevent attacks on his territory: 'Duibhlinn wedded though unwilling with rough-tongued(?) Cathais of the noble shields, Bé Buadha with Tuirgeis of the troops, Bé Binn wedded with Galltor'.[67] Lacey posits that Éichnechán's territory, as the 'lord of fair Fánaid', was largely composed of the area around Gartan, Kilmacrennan and the Fanad Peninsula.[68] Once married, Éichnechán's daughters sailed out of their homeland territory, with their Viking husbands, to an encampment near Carrickabraghy, the location of a Cenél nEógain stronghold in Inishowen. A possible Viking encampment at that site could have survived only with the cooperation of the Cenél nEógain, and we know that they did ally with the Vikings in the 860s, the 870s and again in the mid-tenth century.

One of the daughters, Duibhlinn, was unhappy, and eloped with Cathálan, son of Máel Fábaill of Carrickabraghy, taking with her one thousand ounces of Viking gold. Cathais, 'on account of his sudden loss, went back to Cenn Maghair. He demanded his fair treasure from Ecnechin son of Dalach'.[69] From this, it appears Cenn Maghair (Kinnaweer) was Éichnechán's chief residence. Cathais threatened to plunder all the lands of the Cenél Conaill, but Éichnechán fooled Cathais' men by pretending to prepare an army for a revenge attack against the Cenél nEógain. While sharpening his blade alongside son-in-law Cathais, Éichnechán quickly turned and beheaded him. Éichnechán's army followed his example and massacred the Viking fleet; they 'slew Tuirgeis of the waves and Galltor of the fierce ships [...] "A jest! A jest!" said everyone slaying the bright active Vikings'.[70] Of the 120 ships in the fleet, all of the Viking troops were apparently slaughtered at Cenn Maghair. Duibhlinn, whose marriage to Cathalán was thereafter permitted, returned the Viking gold to her father. Duibhlinn and Cathalán's son Gartnel would later fight alongside the Cenél nEogain king of Ireland, Niall Glúndub, against the Vikings at Mag Feimin. Gartnel, the 'toiseach of Cairrge Brachaidhe', was later killed on the battlefield in 917: 'I grieve that Gartnel son of fair Cathalan has his grave in Munster'.[71]

Ard na scéla, a mheic na ccuach is significant as it provides detail of Viking alliances and failed alliances that may have taken place in Donegal that perhaps were not significant enough to warrant reference in the annals. Furthermore, the source does not contain any obvious exaggeration, except perhaps the wealth of the Vikings and the number of individuals slaughtered.[72]

GRIANÁN OF AILEACH, GREENAN HILL, BURT

At the turn of the tenth century, 'Aileach' was sacked by Vikings, but where exactly is Aileach? Different interpretations and translations present difficulties in citing an exact location. *Chronicon Scotorum* noted that 'Ailech was plundered by the foreigners' in 904.[73] The Annals of the Four Masters had that 'Oileach Frigreann was plundered by the foreigners' in 901.[74] John O'Donovan recorded 'Oileach-Frigreann, otherwise written Aileach-Frigreann, now Elagh, near Lough Swilly, in the barony of Inishowen, and county of Donegal'[75] He cited the *Dinnsenchus*, indicating that the royal fort of Aileach was sometimes called Aileach Frigreinn, from Frigreann, the architect who built it.[76] While many would presume that this refers to the stone fort, Grianán of Ailcach, that lies atop the Greenan Mountain in Donegal, the identification of this exact location is contentious. Richard Warner highlights that this monument is often presumed, incorrectly, to mark the capital of the Cenél nEogain from the sixth until the early twelfth century.[77] Henry Morris believed that the location of Aileach was not the site of the fort, but the nearby townlands of Elaghmore (Derry) and Elaghbeg (Donegal).[78] James Hogan complicated the issue by suggesting that in the late eighth century a common name for the kingdom of the Northern Uí Néill was 'Ailech'.[79] Lacey cited three ancient uses of the name Aileach: first, the name of the stone fort on Greenan Mountain; secondly, from the fifth century onward the name of the homeland territory of Cenél nEogain derived from the site at Elaghmore/Elaghbeg; and thirdly, from c.789 onwards, the name of the over-kingdom of the Northern Uí Néill.[80] Lacey believed that, following the Battle of Cloftech in 789, the Cenél nEógain may have moved their 'headquarters' from Elaghmore to a prehistoric hillfort at the top of Greenan Mountain, in their newly acquired territory. They brought with them the title of their kingdom, Aileach, named after the site at Elaghmore.[81]

Thus, references to the plundering of 'Aileach' could allude to the fort on the Greenan Mountain but, according to Lacey, more likely refer to the territory around the townlands of Elaghmore and Elaghbeg. In any case, the Vikings were targeting the territories belonging to the Cenél nEógain at the turn of the tenth century.[82]

LOUGH FOYLE/INISHOWEN

Around 921, major warfare ensued between the Vikings, under Alcob, and the leadership of the Northern Uí Néill:

> A fleet of the foreigners came into Loch Febail, i.e. Acolb with thirty-two ships. Cennrig was quickly(?) and completely abandoned by them, except for a few who remained behind in it through sloth. Fergal son of Domnall, king of the North, was in hostilities with them, and killed the crew of one of their ships and wrecked the ship and took its booty. Another naval force was at Cenn Magair on the coast of Tír Conaill, i.e. under the son of Uathmarán son of Barid, with twenty ships.[83]

The corresponding reference in the Annals of the Four Masters indicates that Inishowen was also plundered during the strife: 'A fleet of foreigners, consisting of thirty-two ships, at Loch-Feabhail, under Olbh; and Inis-Eoghain was plundered by them […]'.[84] Raghnall Ó Floinn speculated that Cennrig was Dunree Head, on Lough Swilly.[85] Although there is no specific documentary or archaeological evidence for a Viking settlement at Dunree, it may be that a 'short-lived land settlement' existed there.[86] Kinnaweer, in the vicinity of Cranford, north of Kilmacrennan, is on the west side of Mulroy Bay. Downham speculated that a Viking camp existed here.[87] Furthermore, there is

Documentary evidence for Vikings in Co. Donegal

possible evidence for a Viking burial close to Kinnaweer.[88] The king of Tara who died in 710 is named after this area, Congal Cennmagair. Confusingly, there is a reference in the Annals of the Four Masters for a *longphort* there in 1461, however, this by then was more than likely a Gaelic camp. Could the name, though, reference an earlier *longphort* in or near Kinnaweer during the Viking Age?

MUIRCHERTACH AND THE VIKINGS

Also in 921 Muirchertach son of Niall and Aignert son of Murchad defeated the foreigners who invaded Armagh: 'Ard Macha was invaded by the foreigners of Áth Cliath [...] but Muirchertach son of Niall and Aignert son of Murchad came upon the force that had gone north, defeating them, and they left many dead behind'.[89] Almost twenty years later, in 939, Aileach was attacked by Vikings and Muirchertach was captured. The Annals of the Four Masters had: 'Aileach was plundered by the foreigners against Muircheartach, son of Niall; and they took him prisoner, and carried him off to their ships, but God redeemed him from them'.[90]

A few years later, Muirchertach did not escape a second time, and was killed by Vikings: 'Muirchertach son of Niall, heir designate of Ireland, was killed in Áth Firdia by the foreigners of Áth Cliath, and Ard Macha was plundered by the heathens'.[91] The same year, the Ua Canannáin launched an attack on the Cenél nEógain, perhaps because of the power vacuum left by Muirchertach's death: 'a battle-rout was inflicted by Ua Canannáin, by Ruaidrí, on the Cenél nEógain with the foreigners of Loch Febail, in which many fell including Mael Ruanaid son of Flann, heir designate of the North'.[92] The equivalent entry in the Annals of the Four Masters painted a clearer picture: 'A victory was gained at Tracht-Mugha, by Ruaidhri Ua Canannain, over the Cinel-Eoghain and the foreigners of Loch-Feabhail, where three hundred of the Cinel-Eoghain and foreigners were slain, together with Maelruanaidh, son of Flann, heir apparent of the North'.[93] This entry suggested that the Cenél nEógain were allied with the Lough Foyle Vikings against the Ua Canannáin.

Tracht-Mugha could be interpreted as Muff, Co. Donegal, which is situated on the Inishowen Peninsula, at the mouth of the River

Foyle. It is very close to the current border with Co. Derry. Another argument considers that the site in question was Eglinton in Derry. Eglinton was originally called Muff and there is a Muff River and Muff Glen there.[94] Eglinton is only 15km from the Muff in Inishowen. Thus, both of these options are viable. Lacey thinks that Eglinton is the more likely of the two, specifically on a beach nearby the village.[95] Eglinton has since been totally transformed by land reclamation as a result of the building of the railway. While it is difficult to establish where this event took place, it is equally hard to confirm what exactly was the political motivation for the event, and who was allied with whom. It appears that Ruairí Ua Canannáin, who was briefly a very powerful Cenél Conaill king, attempted to take on the Cenél nEógain to restore his kingdom to power, after their defeat in 789.

POSSIBLE SITES OF VIKING ACTIVITY

Rathlin O'Birne

Rathlin O'Birne is situated off the coast of Malinbeg in southwest Co. Donegal. The mainland in the vicinity is rich in medieval remains, while there is a history of monasticism on the island itself. Paul Walsh conceded, however, that 'nothing definite is known of the history of the monastic site on Rathlin O'Birne Island'.[96] The association of the fifth-century St Assicus with this island may be inferred from a reference to him in Patrician sources.[97] An archaeological survey of Rathlin O'Birne confirmed that an early medieval ecclesiastical settlement was established there, but there is no datable evidence for the foundation and abandonment of the monastery. Walsh suggests that because the remains are primitive in nature and because of the association with the fifth-century St Assicus, this church site was founded at the 'very beginnings of Irish monasticism'.[98] Walsh considers that the monastery may have suffered a similar fate to Inishmurray, off the coast of Co. Sligo, which was plundered by Vikings in 795. Lacey believes that the 795 reference to the burning of *Rechru* by the Vikings may refer to Rathlin O'Birne, rather than Rathlin Island off the coast of Co. Antrim.[99] The position of the island would have made it an easy target for sea-raiders, and it is known that the Vikings were active on the west coast of Ireland that year. Viking burials have been discovered on Rathlin Island, but no archaeological evidence for Viking activity has, as yet, been found on Rathlin O'Birne, possibly due to the lack of excavation.[100] It is interesting to note, however, that the place-name Oeeynagall on Rathlin O'Birne in Irish is *Uaigh na Gall*, which translates as the 'Grave of the Foreigners'. In the absence of more specific evidence, Viking presence on Rathlin O'Birne must remain speculation.

Inishbofin

After their initial attacks on *Rechru*, Vikings travelled along the north coast of the country and attacked coastal monasteries in the west, including Inishmurray and Inishbofin. While this Inishbofin is generally believed to be the island off the coast of Co. Galway, Tomás Ó Cannan suggested that the Inishbofin in question may be the island off the Donegal coast between Tory and the mainland.[101] There is no evidence, however, of an early ecclesiastical settlement on the Donegal Inishbofin.[102]

Inishtrahull

Sean Beattie has argued that Inishtrahull, 11km off the coast of the Inishowen Peninsula, was a Viking base.[103] He maintains that there is place-name evidence for Viking activity on the island.[104] This is considered in Chapter 3.

* * *

This chapter has shown that there is a wide range of documentary evidence for Viking activity in Donegal in the ninth and tenth centuries. The majority of the evidence relates to the territories of the Cenél nEógain, which coincides with the archaeological evidence. Four hoards of Viking silver have been unearthed in Inishowen, which is significant, given the rarity of Viking silver hoards in the north-west of Ireland.[105] Graham-Campbell has interpreted the finds as relating to the 921 reference of Alcolb's Viking fleet in the region and suggested that they were deposited during this tumultuous period.[106] Some temporary Viking settlement likely took place in Donegal, but they could not muster enough power to develop settlements in the way that they did in Dublin, Wexford and Waterford. Although the Vikings in Donegal were generally defeated and driven out, they left a longstanding legacy. While never establishing a permanent stronghold in Donegal, Vikings did assimilate into the county's social and political culture, predominantly through intermarriage. This is most evident in language, place-names, surnames and folklore.

3. Viking legacies in Donegal

As seen in Chapters 1 and 2, there is clear archaeological and documentary evidence for the presence of Vikings in Donegal.[1] Perhaps most significant, however, are the striking legacies that remain in cultural memory. Norse legacies are evident in the Irish language in the Donegal Gaeltacht. There are some place-names with possible Old Norse influences, or that relate to Vikings or 'foreigners' in some way. Personal and family names are also prominent indicators of long-lasting Viking legacies in the county, which stemmed originally from Norse-Gael political alliance and intermarriage. Most interesting, however, is the Viking legacy which is evident in folklore and oral history. Charles Doherty has said the following of his own relationship with Viking legacies in Donegal:

> As a young child in the late fifties I played in an old boat that had been beached near Greencastle in Inishowen, Co. Donegal. Years later I heard discussions about those boats by the fishermen in the local pub. They called the boat a 'Drontham' as it sounded to me, otherwise known as the Greencastle Yawl [...] In 1992, a book was published by a man who had sat beside me in class in secondary school, Dónal McPolin, incidentally with a surname that may be Viking in origin since the name Polin was one of those favoured by the Dublin Norse [...] The book was entitled *The Drontheim: forgotten sailing boat of the north Irish coast*. It was only then when I saw the name written down that I realized that the boat I had played in took its name from the local mispronunciation of Trondheim in Norway [...] They were basically a Norwegian boat of the late eighteenth century that was adapted to local conditions along the north-west coast of Ireland, but details in their construction show a clear ancestry going back to the classic Viking ships of the eighth and ninth centuries [...] Our Norse links have not quite disappeared and in this small way I feel a special link with the Norsemen of our past.[2]

Doherty's fascinating anecdote perfectly summarizes the extent of the Viking legacy in Donegal: it is all around, in names, in material culture and in folktales. The following will emphasize the Viking heritage of Donegal.

NORSE LOANWORDS IN IRISH

The Irish language highlights Viking legacies because of the Norse loanwords that survive and are still used by Irish speakers today. The Donegal Gaeltacht, the second-highest populated Gaeltacht after Galway, has a population of 23,346 Irish speakers who commonly use the remaining Scandinavian-Irish loanwords in their day-to-day vocabulary.[3] By Scandinavian, we mean the language brought to Ireland by the Vikings and called Old Norse in current linguistic usage. David Greene argued that 'it is impossible to say when linguistic contacts began', but when we read that an Irish king allied himself with the Vikings in the ninth century to attack a neighbouring dynasty, we must assume that negotiations were achieved by bilingual speakers. The same can be said for Viking and Irish merchants undertaking trade or bargaining; thus, bilingualism was the prerequisite for word borrowing.[4] The loanwords people use, moving from one language to the other, offer a glimpse into the identities of the people who were borrowing these words, those at 'the frontier of language contact'.[5] Loanwords needed Norse speakers to utter them and Gaelic speakers to adopt them, highlighting the relationships that formed between the Irish and the Vikings.

The extent of Old Norse loanwords has often been overlooked (table 1), with Magne Oftedal and Ó Corráin arguing for fewer than fifty surviving words and Greene considering fewer than twenty.[6] Roderick McDonald believes that there are approximately 460 likely loanwords in Irish, Scots Gaelic and Manx that have been borrowed from Old Norse, and a further 170 that are uncertain.[7] An analysis of these loanwords provides information on the various social affiliations and community activities that arose from Viking settlement in Ireland, especially when the words are considered in the context of archaeological evidence.[8] Viking settlement and activity in the west occurred during a time of political and economic reorganization between Dublin, York and the Hebrides. Opportunities arose for

Viking legacies in Donegal

people to transform roles, pastimes, activities and identities, as specific and local needs demanded.[9] Old Norse-speaking communities in Hiberno-Norse towns survived until the Anglo-Norman conquest, after which they were ultimately assimilated, legally and culturally, into the English colony in Ireland.[10]

Table 1. Selection of Old Norse loanwords found in Irish

Irish	Old Norse	English
ábua	hábora	oarport
accaire	akkeri	anchor
bát	bát	boat
beirling	berling	warship
bróg	brók	shoe
cnap	knappr	button
erell / iarla	jarl	earl
langa	langa	long
leagadh	leggja	to lower (sail)
lunnta	hlunnr	oar-handle
margadh	markadr	market
matal	móttull	cloak
pónair	baunir	bean
punnan	binda	sheaf
scibeadh	skipa	to equip a ship
scilling	skilling	shilling
scúta	skúta	warship
sess	sess	seat
sreng	strengr	rope
stag	stag	stay
tochta	tophta	thwart
trosc	throskr	cod

(source: Anne-Christine Larsen, 'The exhibition: the Vikings in Ireland' in Anne-Christine Larsen (ed.), *The Vikings in Ireland* (Roskilde, 2001), p. 145)

It might be anticipated that the Irish words describing the Viking invaders would have been borrowed from Old Norse, but this is not the case. Initially they are described as *gaill*, from the Latin *gentes* meaning 'pagans', and the Latin *nortmanni*, 'northmen', usually taken from English sources.[11] Later, however, *Danair* 'Danes' comes from

Old Norse *Danir*, and *Dannmargg* 'Denmark' are first attested in a text attributed to the eleventh century.[12] The most debated Irish descriptors for Vikings and the Viking homelands are of course *Lothlind*, *Laithlind*, later *Lochlann* and *Lochlannach*. Greene states that it is possible that the earlier forms denote Viking Scotland, or some Viking maritime stronghold, while the later terms undoubtedly refer to Norway and Norse Vikings, by the twelfth century.[13] Others, such as Colmán Etchingham, argued that it is possible that all the terms denote Norway or Scandinavia.[14] The identification of *Iruath* with Norway is made in Middle Irish documents such as *Acallam na Senórach* and currently the *Ioruaidh* of Modern Irish denotes Norway. *Lochlannach* can mean Norse, Scandinavian, Norseman or marauder. *Gall*, as discussed in the introduction to this study, continues to describe 'foreigners' in Modern Irish.[15]

What Old Norse loanwords in Irish are still spoken? The earliest identifiable Norse loanword is *erell* (Old Irish), *iarla* (Modern Irish) from *jarl* (Old Norse).[16] This, and other Old Norse loanwords in Irish fall into clearly delineated categories. The categories in which one can find most Old Norse loanwords are the following, as set out by McDonald: 'skins, clothing and materials', 'social status, roles and responsibilities', 'people and their component parts', 'aggression and warfare', 'maritime activities and equipment', 'exchange, trade and payments' and 'buildings and sites'. These categories were formed in comparison with loanwords found in Scottish Gaelic, where it was found that Norse loanwords relating to 'farming, commodities and products' were similarly found in both languages.[17]

From analysing these loanword categories, we learn that the types of Old Norse words that were borrowed into Irish reflect daily life in Viking-Age Ireland. Words relating to 'farming, commodities and products', 'exchange, trade and payments' and 'skins, clothing and materials' emphasize the importance of the market-place and the exchange of goods needed for survival such as food and clothing. Words that fall into the categories of 'social status, roles and responsibilities', 'buildings and sites' and 'aggression and warfare' seem to arise from changing social, economic and political roles in Hiberno-Norse Ireland.

A significant category of loanwords, 'maritime activities and equipment', deals with shipbuilding and seamanship. Old Norse survived in Dublin and some other larger settlements until at least the time of the Anglo-Norman invasion, and for a period after. Some Irish place-names were translated from Norse into English, such as Limerick which clearly derives from the Old Norse *Hylmrekr*, not the Irish *Luimneach*.[18] Modern Irish certainly contains Old Norse loanwords, which are still spoken by the native Irish speakers in their everyday vocabulary. For example, the word *punnan*, meaning 'sheaf' in Modern Irish, derives from Old Norse *bundan*. Interestingly, there is no trace of it in Scottish Gaelic.[19]

NORSE-GAEL INTERMARRIAGE

In the mid-ninth century, some Viking settlements in Ireland, notably Dublin, began to extend 'their ties with the native population of Ireland, establishing political, social and economic links with their neighbours and becoming very much a part of the Irish landscape'.[20] Dublin was the most important of the Viking settlements in Ireland. The leaders of Dublin, named in the sources beginning in 853, were first described as three chieftains, and soon after as three kings. This indicates that Dublin was very successful within a generation of its foundation. One of the Dublin kings, Óláfr, had married into an Irish royal family by 862, forging a political and military alliance with Áed Findliath, Cenél nEógain king of the Northern Uí Néill. Later, however, Áed would turn against his ally Óláfr. Perhaps it was when he became high-king of Ireland that the Dublin Viking king was transformed from ally to threat.[21] The breakdown of this alliance is signalled by Áed Findliath routing Viking bases in the north in 866 and his confrontation with an alliance of Vikings, the Uí Néill of Brega and the Leinstermen in 868.[22]

The Gall-Ghaedhil 'Viking-Irish' were first mentioned in Irish sources in 856. As discussed in Chapter 2, Áed Findliath inflicted a great rout on the Gall-Ghaedhil in Glenelly in 856 and a vast number of them were slaughtered by him. The same year, the Gall-Ghaedhil allied with Máel Sechnaill, a Clann Colmáin king of Meath and the overking of the Uí Néill, against whom Áed Findliath was rebelling. In 857 Óláfr and Ívar of Dublin defeated the king of Munster, and his Gall-Ghaedhil allies. The annalists record activity by the Gall-

Ghaedhil for the last time in 858, when Cearbhall mac Dunlang of Ossory with his ally Ívar of Dublin defeated the combined forces of the Cenél Fiachach and the Gall-Ghaedhil.[23]

The Gall-Ghaedhil were a group of Scandinavian and Gaelic mercenaries working together. It is hard to deduce whether the Gall-Ghaedhil referred to in the annals are one group, or a number of factions. The geographical origins of the Gall-Ghaedhil as a singular cohort or multiple groups are unknown. If in 857 and 858 the Dublin Vikings Óláfr and Ívar fought against the Gall-Ghaedhil, then they are unlikely to have any relation with Dublin. The Fragmentary Annals describe the Gall-Ghaedhil as the Irish 'fosterchildren' of the Vikings. This text, as discussed previously, is known for exaggeration, but noble Irish children were sometimes fostered with Viking settlers. In 872, Bairid, leader of the 'Dark Foreigners', is described as the 'fosterfather of the king's son'. The king in question was Áed Findliath, with whom peaceful relations were made to propagate Viking survival in the north.[24] This foster alliance would later form blood links between the Cenél nEógain and Bairid.

The term Gall-Ghaedhil came to be used generally to describe families of Hiberno-Norse origin. Meanwhile, in Scotland, a group also called the Gall-Ghaedhil emerged, and settled in Galloway in the latter part of the ninth century. The Irish Gall-Ghaedhil occupied large parts of Cumberland, Westmoreland, Lancashire and West Rising in the tenth century, and were largely Norse-speaking but with some Gaelic speakers.[25] The Gall-Ghaedhil gave rise to a class of mercenaries known as the *Gallóglaigh* or 'Gallowglasses'. They played a prominent military role in fourteenth-, fifteenth- and sixteenth-century Ireland, thus giving rise to politically important families, which had their origins in Norse-Gaelic intermarriage. There is a legacy of gallowglass surnames in Ulster, particularly Donegal, which will be discussed below.

ONOMASTIC EVIDENCE FOR VIKINGS IN DONEGAL: PERSONAL NAMES
AND SURNAMES

It is often claimed that Ruairí Ua Canannáin, who died *c*.950, was the first person in Ireland to have a surname. Family names or surnames became common in Ireland during the reign of Brian Bóruma, at the beginning of the eleventh century. Several families adopted the names of fathers, grandfathers, or even went back several generations to choose a remote ancestor who was an acknowledged authority. It appears that the most distinguished surnames in Ireland were the names of progenitors who flourished in the tenth or early eleventh century, by prefixing 'Ó' or 'Mac' to denote 'grandson of', or 'son of', respectively. After some time, both extended to signify any male descendant.[26]

The Irish began borrowing Scandinavian personal names from an early period. Examples are Amlaib, Dubgall, Gofraid, Ímar, Lochlainn, Magnus, Sitriuc and Ragnall. The earliest records of Scandinavian personal names in Irish sources are the names of Viking leaders who had been active in the country.[27] By the end of the ninth century, Irish names were being borrowed by Hiberno-Norse families. The son of a Viking chief had the Irish name Uathmaran ('the awesome one'), son of Bairid. He married the daughter of Domnall mac Aeda, king of Ailech, and they had a son who was given the Norse name Sichfraid. Thus, this individual appears in the Annals of Ulster in 933 with the Hiberno-Norse hybrid name Sichfraidh mac Uathmarain.[28] As previously indicated, Bairid was the Viking fosterfather of Áed Findliath's (king of Ailech and later high-king of Ireland) children, which may be the origin of the link between the Cenél nEógain and Viking families.

It is well known that the Irish adopted Norse personal names, which still survive in present-day Donegal, surnames such as M(a)cManus and M(a)cAuley/M(a)cAuliffe. M(a)cManus is thought to derive from *Mac Mághnais*, which, coming from the popular Norse name Magnus, means 'son of Magnus'. M(a)cAuley/M(ac)Auliffe translates as 'son of Amhlaibh' and possibly derives from *Amlaíb*, the Irish translation of the Norse name *Óláfrr*. This was the name of one of the Dublin kings in the ninth century, who at one time had an alliance with the Cenél nEógain in the Northern Uí Néill and married the daughter of King Áed Findliath. Other Donegal surnames may also have Viking origins. McPolin, as indicated by Doherty in the introduction to this chapter, could be derived from the popular Norse name *Polin*. Grimes is thought to come from the Norse personal name *Grimr*, a surname that possibly came to Ireland from the Danelaw. Reynolds/Randles from *Mac Raghnall* could derive from the Norse name *Ragnall* (son of

Ragnall). Grourke/Groarke/O'Rourke from *Mag Ruairc* may have its origins in the Norse name *Hrothkekr* (son of Hrothkekr). McBirney/McBurney, an Ulster-Scots surname, may derive from Norse *Bjorn* to mean 'son of Bjorn'.[29]

The possible Viking origin of some common Donegal surnames, such as McLoughlin, deriving from *Mac Lochlann*, and Higgens or Higney, deriving from *O hUiginn*, have been disputed among scholars. Despite the aforementioned association of the word *Lochlann* with Vikings, either Norse or Scottish, *Mac Lochlann* is judged by Fergus Mac Giolla Easpaig to be a Cenél nEógain surname, with no relation to Vikings.[30] Greene considered Ó Loughlin and McLoughlin to originate in the personal name *Lochlainn* but agreed that it was not derived from the Norse.[31]

Carl Marstrander and Eoin MacNeill considered Uiginn to derive from Old Norse *víkingr*. Middle Irish *ucíng*, meaning 'Viking', is not attested before the twelfth century and was usually used in the context of maritime expedition, or fleet, representing *víking* not *víkingr*.[32] Although, if you consider that surnames first became hereditary in the eleventh century, families in the twelfth century may still have been forging their familial identities. By this time, the word *ucíng*, denoting 'Viking', may have appeared and been an attractive ancestral namesake. Marstrander rejected the derivation of Scots Gaelic *úig* 'cove' from Old Norse *vík*, suggesting that it should be compared with the Irish *uaig*, meaning 'sea-cave'.[33] The Irish word *úig* is found in northern Irish, a sign of potential Scottish influence. Oftedal rejected the comparison of *úig* with *uaig*, and firmly identifies it with *vík*.[34] Greene agreed that the evidence is in favour of accepting that *Víkingr* is Uiginn, despite semantic and phonetic difficulties.[35]

As mentioned above, the *Gallóglaigh*, a class of Norse-Gael mercenaries, gave rise to a number of important families in Ulster, especially Donegal, whose origins can be traced to Viking and Gael intermarriage. MacAilín (meaning 'Mac Allen' or 'Son of Allen', with modern day variations McCallion, Campbell) of Inishowen are likely a branch of the MacAilín of Galloway, who returned to Ireland to work as *gallóglaigh* for the O'Donnell.[36] MacSuibhne (MacSweeney, Sweeney) are another Scottish gallowglass family who settled in Donegal at the beginning of the fourteenth century to work as mercenaries for the O'Donnell chieftans. They claimed to have remote Irish ancestry from a Cenél nEógain king who died in 1036, and while this may be a 'convenient fabrication', Mac Giolla Easpaig cited W.D.H. Sellar who argued that it was possible.[37] The historic name of Milford, a town north of Letterkenny, is Ballynagalloglagh (Irish: *Baile na nGallóglach*), a place-name that indicates a considerable number of gallowglass families may have settled in that area and provided the name of the town.

ONOMASTIC EVIDENCE FOR VIKINGS IN DONEGAL: TOPONYMY

The primary aim of toponymy, the study of place-names as an auxiliary science, is to investigate an aspect of social psychology: 'how groups of men down the ages designated their homes, villages, fields, districts etc., and the mystical or realistic manifestations of the popular mind evident from this proceeding'.[38] Ethnologically and historically, toponymy aids the study of migrations, colonizations and conquests, and can help the researcher form conclusions about their character and extent. Accurately interpreted place-names can be clues for the archaeologist, indicating where one can seek fossils of human geography.[39]

The Vikings who raided and settled in Ireland made a relatively small impression on the place-names of the country,[40] Yet their legacy has endured in towns and cities such as Dublin, Waterford and Wexford. The majority of Old Norse place-names in Ireland are on the south east coastline. The lost *Ulfreksfjorðr*, along with Strangford, Carlingford, Waterford and Wexford are examples of names with the Norse ending *-fjorðr*, meaning 'fjord' or 'sea inlet'.[41] Wicklow and Arklow contain the Old Norse element *ló* 'grassy meadow'. A number of other place-names contain Viking personal names, i.e. Ballyfermot, Ballygunner, Curtlestown (*Baile mhic Thorcail*) and Ballally (*Baile meic Amhlaibh*). The Irish *baile* 'settlement' indicates that the names were coined by the Irish, but referred to Thormoth, Gunnar and the sons of Thorkel and Óláfr respectively.[42] There are more Irish place-names which have Norse origins, including Fingal, Oxmanstown, Ireland's Eye, Leixlip and others (table 2).

Dún na nGall, 'Fort of the Foreigners'?

Table 2. Selection of Norse-influenced place-names in Ireland

Ballyfermot	Baile Thormoth	Thormoth's by
Ballygunner	Baile Gunnar	Gunnar's by
Curtlestown	Baile mhic Thorcail	Thorkil's son's by
Ballally	Baile meic Amhlaibh	Olaf's son's by
Ballytruckle	Baile Thorcail	Thorkel's by
Lambay	Lamba-ey	Lamb island
Dalkey	Dalk-ey	Thorn island
Howth	Höfthi	Headland
Strangford	Strangr fjördr	Strong (current)
Carlingford	Kerling fjördr	Old woman (The Three Nuns)
Wexford	Ueig fjördr	The waterlogged one
Waterford	Vedr fjördr	Windy fjord
Arklow	Arnketil lö	Arnketil's grassy meadow
Wicklow	Vík lö	Pasture by the creek

(source: Larsen, 'The exhibition', p. 145)

Old Norse-influenced, or Viking-related place-names in Donegal are difficult to identify. In the introduction to this study, Donegal as *Dún na nGall* – 'Fort of the Foreigners', was discussed. Patrick Weston Joyce supported the theory that the 'foreigners' in question were Vikings: 'The Danes had a settlement there before the Anglo-Norman invasion [...] the fortress of the *Galls* or foreigners'.[43] This view is also backed by Patrick McKay: 'the foreigners referred to are likely to have been Vikings who are known to have been active in Donegal bay in the ninth century'.[44] Although *gall* came to signify the English by the sixteenth century, two previous names were recorded from the fifteenth and thirteenth centuries, *Áth na nGall* and *Thethnegall* (likely *Teach na nGall*) respectively. Donal Mac Giolla Easpaig believed the evidence suggests that the 'foreigners' in question belonged to a period preceding the Anglo-Norman invasion, between the ninth and thirteenth centuries and 'were in all probability Vikings'.[45] He goes on to say that it is 'not unlikely that these Vikings would have established a number of semi-permanent trading settlements [...] Donegal offered a site that would have been attractive to Viking traders in the ninth and tenth centuries'.[46] As mentioned earlier, Ó Canann has also considered that the mound at Doonan Rock could represent the first archaeological confirmation of a Viking settlement on the River Eske not far from Donegal town.[47]

As discussed earlier, Vikings were experts in seafaring, thus, were most accustomed to island, sea inlet and coastal territories. We must first consider Donegal's islands for Norse onomastic evidence. Willie Smith, quoted in an article by Nollaig Ó Muraile, argued that there had been an underestimation of the Norse contribution to Donegal place-names, and suggested that the toponymy of Tory Island has in some way been misrepresented.[48] Beattie believes Inishtrahull was a Viking settlement, based on onomastic evidence. The place-names 'Stacknafeola' and 'Stacknamara' on the island could be derived from Old Norse. In Old Norse, *stakkr* is a haystack so the name applies to a headland like a haystack.[49] Furthermore, a group of rocks off the Inishtrahull coast are called 'Skerries', and like Skerries, Co. Dublin, could come from *scéirí* – the Gaelicization of Old Norse *sceir* meaning 'reefs'. If we consider Beattie's *stakkr* as the basis for Stackamore, Stackarory, Stackanrelagh, Stackacrave, Stackanbarna and Stackanaglassan on Arranmore Island, this could reflect Viking settlement there. Scalpnadinga, also on Arranmore, could derive from Old Norse *skálpr* meaning 'sheath', and 'dinga' may have some relation to Old Norse *þing* meaning 'assembly'. Other Donegal islands have place-names that reference *gall*, 'foreigners'. For example, Loghmagheranagall (*Loch Mhachaire na nGall* – The Lake of the Foreigner's Plain), Gola Island and Illannagall (*Oileán na nGall* the Island of the Foreigners), Eighter Island. As we saw earlier, on Rathlin O'Birne there is a place called Ooeynagall (*Uaigh na nGall* 'Grave of the Foreigners').

Evidence of Viking activity is to be found at coastal areas around Co. Donegal. There are Old Norse place-names at Malin Head, including Ineuran Bay, meaning 'small sheltered harbour', and Scheildrén Mór and Scheildrén Beag, meaning 'shield'.[50] The Scheildrén are sea stacks at the north-western tip of the headland, previously called 'Skildrenmore' and 'Skildrenbeg' on Ordnance Survey six-inch maps. Sheephaven Bay may derive from Old Norse *Skip Havn*, where Sheephaven is an anglicization of the Norse name.[51] Off Rinmore Point, there is a rocky island called 'Flughog'. This could come from Old Norse *haug/haugr* meaning 'mound' or 'hill'. Finally, there are some possible Norse-influenced or Viking-related place-names inland. Aughagault, *Achadh na nGall* is usually translated as 'the English Field'. *Gall*, however, can be interpreted as 'foreigner', which in some cases refers to Vikings in Irish territories. Aughagault is situated in the barony of Raphoe south, where a Viking silver hoard was found. Additionally, there is Lisgall (*Lios Gall* – Fort of the Foreigners) in Inishowen where three hoards were found ('Northwest Inishowen', Roosky and Carrowmore). Carricknagall Island is in Culdaff, where local lore maintains that Vikings butchered animals at *Pairc na gCraicinn*, Bunagee. Finally, there is a place called 'Norway' in Clonmany, also near Roosky.[52]

VIKINGS IN DONEGAL FOLKLORE AND ORAL HISTORY

> It would be rash to deny the existence of famous personages, merely because mysterious or incredible exploits are ascribed to them [...] Mythic characters are to be found in the early history of every country; but the judicious historian of the present day inclines to the opinion that these were real individuals, remarkable for some great quality, and whom tradition has invested with a supernatural glory.[53]

James MacGrady here considers the legacy of mythological characters such as Finn McCool, but his words can be applied in a similar sense to the Viking legacy in folklore. Although oral histories are subject to exaggeration, a weakness that must be considered, it is possible that a grain of truth can be detected. The author has used Dúchas.ie, an online resource that digitizes material from the National Folklore Collection, to find folkloric material relating to Co. Donegal. A number of keyword searches were carried out, and Donegal consistently appeared strongly in these searches (table 3). Donegal is a large county, thus providing more scope for folklore collection. Perhaps oral storytelling survived longer in this north-western county, on the periphery of Irish life. But this does not explain why Donegal has such a significant Viking oral history when the county has been scarcely mentioned in any historiographical considerations of the Vikings in Ireland.

Table 3. Folkloric evidence for Vikings in modern Co. Donegal

Keyword searched on Dúchas.ie	Total number of entries featuring that keyword	Number of counties corresponding to total entries	Number of entries pertaining to Co. Donegal	Position in rank (most entries to fewest entries)
'Vikings'	6	5	1	2nd=
'Norse'	18	11	2	2nd=
'Lochlannach'	27	6	10	1st
'Lochlannaigh'	71	11	18	1st=
'Danish'	c.300	25	26	3rd
'Danes'	c.2,000	26	142	4th

(source: National Folklore Collection, digitised on Dúchas.ie)

FOLKTALES: DRUMHOLM

Four Donegal folklore tales refer to the townland of Drumholm or Drimholm, the local names for Drumhome (Irish: *Droim Thuama* meaning 'Ridge of the Grave-Mound').[54] Three entries refer to a battle taking place there between the Irish and the 'Danes'. One tale indicates that the Danes were defeated, while another says that the Danes won. It is said that a 'thousand were killed' and that 'there is a large height in which they are buried'.[55] Two of the tales imply that once the battle was over, they began to 'drum home', and this became the name of the townland in remembrance. One Drumholm tale also refers to the discovery of skeletal remains:

> In the townland of Drimholm about two miles from Ballintra a discovery was made by two men who were preparing the land for spring cropping in the year 1936. They came upon two large flag stones [...] The men began to raise the stones and when one was raised it disclosed a grave in which a skeleton of a person lay. This person had flaxen hair which when touched crumpled away. The second stone having been lifted disclosed a skeleton similar to the first [...] the skeletons were of two Danes who were killed in the fight and buried there.[56]

It is hard to imagine either Viking or Irish warriors 'drumming home', but it is interesting that the local name for the place 'Drumholm', when spelt in such a manner, has the Norse ending *holme*, meaning an island or reclaimed marshy area of land. In one folktale, Drumholm is described as a 'potatoes marsh'.[57] Earthen mounds on the surrounding hills of Drumholm are described by one collector as 'Danish forts', although 'they are believed to be the work of the Irish, and to have been constructed anterior to the Danish period'.[58] This collector could be implying that Vikings took control of Irish monuments, or perhaps lodged in those which had fallen into disuse. Whether there is any truth in the folklore, there is a clear Viking legacy in the Drumholm townland.

FOLKTALES: DANISH BATTLES

A Donegal folktale describes a battle between the native Irish and the Vikings:

> Near to the town of Buncrana in the peninsula of Inishowen at a spot where a river flows into the sea there once stood a castle [...] a party of the marauders landed on the shores of Lough Swilly near to the mouth of this little river and at once went to attack the castle [...] the next day was the 1st of May so according to custom the chief ordered a Mayfire to be put up outside his castle on May eve. Next day when the Danes saw this they thought it was a signal of surrender from the Irish. They came up to the castle unarmed. The Irish fell upon them and killed them all.[59]

Another folktale describes the ruinous castle in Faugher, Clondahorky, saying that it was 'built about the eighth century by the O'Boyles' and that 'an attack made on this castle by the Danes but they were defeated by O'Boyle and his army'.[60] The fortified house and its surrounding bawn were built during the Plantation of Ulster. The original castle on this site was reputedly built for Turlough Roe O'Boyle *c.*1611, but, it is possible that ancestors of the O'Boyle family, of the Northern Uí Néill, had a site of significance here during the Viking Age. Furthermore, a fragment of a Viking-Age silver ingot was found at Murroe, Clondahorky.[61]

Viking legacies in Donegal

FOLKTALES: DANISH FORTS AND DANISH TREASURE

Often said to be protected by a whistling eel, a witch or a small red man, these tales refer to treasures or gold left behind by the 'Danes'. Many of the stories also refer to 'Danish Forts', seemingly hillforts or ringforts that were attributed to Vikings. Hillforts are also known from Scandinavia, while a small number of Viking ring-fortresses (trelleborgs) were erected from the tenth century.[62] The *suggestio falsi* of 'Danish Forts' in Ireland had been inherited from medieval antiquarianism, which considered the 'Danes' as ancient invaders of Ireland. This notion, propagated by Giraldus Cambrensis and William Molyneux, proved extremely difficult to dislodge.[63] Nevertheless, Viking silver hoards have been discovered within Irish habitation sites. At Roosky, four silver arm-rings were discovered hidden in the wall of a cashel. Before the discovery, local lore implied that a Dane was buried within this enclosure.[64] Roosky is an example of archaeological evidence coinciding with folklore. This also indicates that Viking silver hoards in Donegal either ended up in Irish hands and were thus deposited for protection in their native settlements, or that Viking invaders had taken control of native sites.

Two folktales describe the 'Danish' presence at Castlecommon, Killybegs. One says that 'One day, the Danes had to leave Castlecommon in a great hurry because their watchman had seen some great ships coming into Killybegs and they were afraid of being taken prisoner. When leaving they could not take the gold with them, therefore they hid it in the tunnel'.[65] A tunnel could be interpreted as a souterrain. One example of a Viking hoard found within a souterrain is the Lurgabrack silver hoard. Another folktale describes Castlebawn, where a 'large grey stone, the circumference of which is about one hundred ft and whose height is about forty ft, is said to mark the spot [...] (where the Vikings) were supposed to hide their gold'.[66] This is reminiscent of the Carrowmore silver hoard, discovered underneath a large flat stone.

One folklore collector recalled a number of forts, in Drimnasillagh, Kilraine, Letterilly and Strangalough: 'it is said that these were built by Danish kings, and when these kings were leaving they hid gold in the foundations of these forts, and some of them retired under the forts themselves'.[67] This tale again suggests the possibility of hoards being deposited within forts, going as far as to suppose that Vikings have been buried within them too. A folklore collector described gold hidden at a 'Danish Fort' in Cnóc Mór (Crockmore), Rosguill, after the Vikings were 'driven away by the Irish after a skirmish'. Locals attested that 'a foreign ship arrived at Dooey and anchored close by. Some of the crew came ashore and went to the Danish fort [...], some of the local people saw them returning to their ships carrying parcels with them which were believed to have been gold'.[68] Previously, we discussed the importance of the Rosguill promontory during the Viking Age, and this folktale attests to that.

Some folktales refer to 'Danish' finds. Two stories reference Drumkeelin, near Mountcharles, and a find of 'Danish coins of great value' in the foundations of a 'Danish Castle' in the Drumkeelin quarry while erecting a machinery plant.[69] The only known hoard of Anglo-Saxon coins was found in Burt, 75km away from Mountcharles, but similarly found during the construction of the Letterkenny railway. At Carricknahorna, a spearhead was found by a local man in a fort of 'Danish construction'.[70] After the sword, the most common weapon to be recovered from Viking burial contexts is the spear, however, there is no way of confirming if this was indeed a Viking-Age spearhead.[71] One folklore collector recalls that in Cruckrooskey, Glenagannon, three men who, during turf-cutting, came upon 'a wooden barrel about two feet in height and one foot broad full of Danish butter'. This undoubtedly refers to a find of bog butter, a phenomenon not particularly common in Donegal. Radiocarbon dating has shown bog butter was buried in Ireland from the Bronze Age up until the late eighteenth century. Chris Synnott gave the most likely explanation for the burying of butter as preservation, with a possible motivation of hiding butter during Viking invasions.[72]

Although most of the folktales refer to 'Danish'-owned forts, or treasures left behind by 'Danes', some mention the native Irish. One tale tells of a 'crock of gold hidden by Danes (or Irish during Danish raids) in an underground cave at the mouth of Lough Foyle'.[73] Another tells of the fort at Tubber: 'Long ago when the Danes were invading Ireland the Irish people built this fort to protect themselves from the Danes'.[74] One goes as far as to say that the Danes stole Irish treasures and hid them in Ballymore Hill, near Ards Strand: 'The Danish robbers took our gold, they oftimes did before, and now it's hid among the caves'.[75] This is significant, as the majority of historians who dealt with Viking hoards found in Donegal have speculated that they were hidden in Irish sites by Irish hands.

FOLKTALES: DANISH BURIALS AND GRAVES

Near Ballintra, a folklore tale attests to the digging up of bones: 'there was a large flat stone over him, and his bones were down under his head' in 'a place like a king's grave which was shaped like a box'.[76] The same folklore tale indicates that another individual was digging elsewhere and 'found a man with yellow hair' who was speculated to be a 'Dane'.[77] Another story pertains to Culdaff, where two large flat stones were uncovered: 'After a time one of them was raised and a rectangular chamber was disclosed underneath. In it lay a skeleton with long flaxen hair and when touched it crumbled into dust [...] the skeleton of a tall man like a Dane with long hair and it in waves'.[78] Two things can be drawn from these examples. First, the stereotypical portrayal of a Viking in Donegal folklore is a tall man with 'yellow', wavy hair, a typical image of north Germanic peoples. Second, the burial chambers described appear to be cist graves, small stone coffin-like boxes mostly datable to the Bronze Age. Simple unprotected graves were most common in Scandinavia (except in the case of high-status burials), however, a cist grave discovered at Kinnegar beach may be associated with a Viking bronze ringed-pin, discussed in Chapter 1.

FOLKTALES: CAVES AND TUNNELS

A number of folktales in Donegal describe Vikings in conjunction with caves, tunnels and underground passageways. These could be interpreted as souterrains – underground chambers found widely distributed across Ireland and dating to the period c.750 to c.1250. Souterrains vary in form from simple single chambers, possibly for storage, to very complex multi-chamber versions, which appear as defensive structures.[79] Richard Warner suggested that this was in response to Viking raids, as a short-term hiding place for people and goods.[80] It is likewise possible that Vikings invaded or made use of abandoned Irish settlement sites. Thus, there are two possibilities for the deposition of a hoard in a souterrain, such as at Lurgabrack. First, the Irish may have obtained the silver through raiding, trading or gift exchange, and stored it for safe keeping in the souterrain. Second, a Viking presence may have taken over the habitation site and hidden the silver in the souterrain for safety. In either scenario, the rightful owner did not return to reclaim these objects for whatever reason.

One folktale describes a 'Dane's Cave' which leads from Rosapenna to Doe Castle and that they 'used to come out and make raids on the people'.[81] The same tale also describes a cave attributed to Danes at Doe Castle, situated alongside a 'Danes graveyard' where all those who died during the Battle of Mislack were buried.[82] No further information on the 'Battle of Mislack' can be obtained by the author, but in the context of the story it seems to describe a battle between the Vikings and the Irish. On a hill called 'Skeagey' in Glenswilly a 'Dane's Cave' is mentioned which has a 'pipe or drain [...] used for making beer from heather. The stones inside the pipe are blackened, as if by smoke from a fire'.[83] The making of heather beer by Vikings is a common trope in Irish and Scottish folklore and is mentioned repeatedly in the samples pertaining to Donegal.[84] The reference to blackened stones in a pipe or trench could describe a fulacht fiadh, a stone-lined cooking pit which dates predominantly to the Bronze Age. Some archaeologists suspect that the fulacht fiadh was actually used for brewing, so perhaps there is some connection or association between this usage and the folkloric notion of Viking heather brewing.[85]

* * *

To summarize, there is a significant Viking legacy in Co. Donegal that has survived into the twenty-first century. It is visible in the Irish language, spoken in the Donegal Gaeltacht, and in some of the county's place-names. Peaceful relations and intermarriage between Scandinavians and Irish are reflected in personal names and family names associated with the county. Most significantly, the Viking legacy has remained steadfast in the county's folktales. Vikings in Donegal were said to have built forts and tunnels for means of escape, hiding treasure and worship, battled the native Irish, made heather beer and butter and, while we cannot conclusively say if there is any historical accuracy to this, these legacies assuredly exist in Donegal's oral culture.

Conclusion

Substantial evidence for Viking activity in Donegal has been uncovered. While the evidence seems to point to a short-lived Viking presence in Donegal, we cannot claim to know the full story. Figure 8 is a map of the archaeological, documentary and possible place-name evidence across modern Co. Donegal. From this, it is clear that there are distinct concentrations of evidence with few outliers.

The confirmed Viking archaeological findings are concentrated in the north/north-east of Donegal, around the Inishowen Peninsula and the Sheephaven Bay area. A Viking presence in these areas is further attested by place-name evidence, which shows possible Old Norse influence, and documentary evidence that describes encounters between the Irish and Vikings, particularly in the areas around Lough Foyle and Lough Swilly. Furthermore, the majority of the archaeological evidence dates from $c.850$ to 950, roughly coinciding with the majority of the documentary evidence. The Burt and Lurgabrack finds comprise the only identifiable post-950 evidence, which broadly indicates potential Viking movement from the north-east to the west and north-west of the county. Lurgabrack and Rinnaraw, together, may indicate that this coastal area of Donegal shared some cultural traditions with Scottish Vikings. The archaeological evidence may prove the failure of the Viking colonies in Co. Donegal, as some of the silver hoards were found in Irish habitation sites. There is evidence for only one possible Viking-type house, at Rinnaraw, also near Sheephaven. Conversely, the finding of Viking artefacts in Irish settlement types could indicate that Vikings adopted abandoned sites in Co. Donegal, or (temporarily) evicted the natives for their personal use. This notion is furthered by folktales that describe 'Danish forts' across the landscape of the county. Archaeological investigation of some of these sites may help to clarify this.

The documentary evidence is strikingly concentrated in the north-east of Co. Donegal, with one major outlier: Assaroe, at the

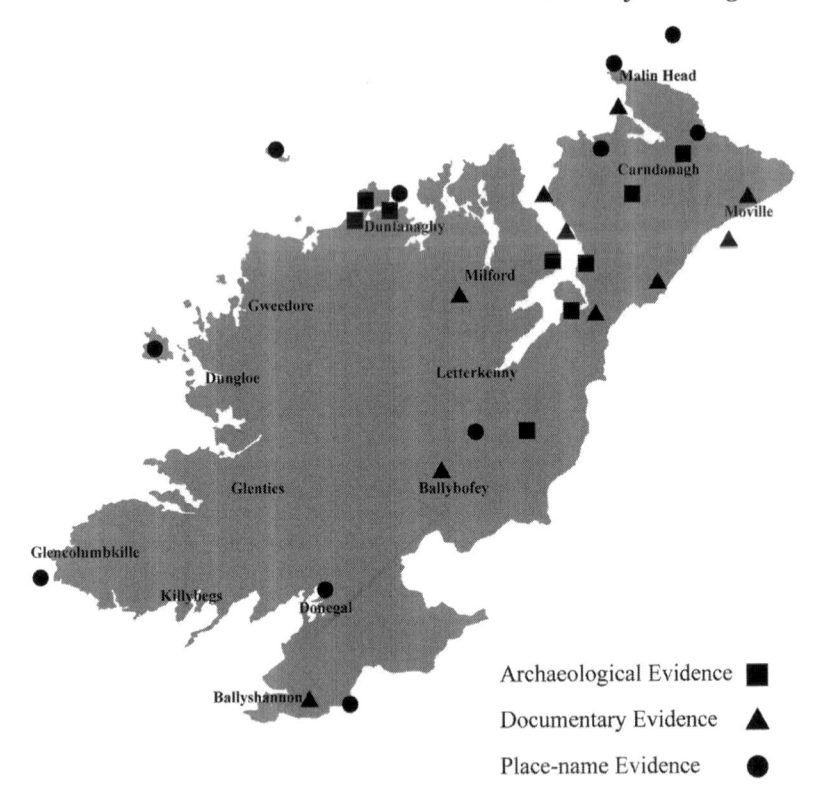

8. Map of the archaeological, documentary and place-name evidence for Vikings in Donegal

very southern tip of the county. Assaroe is not an outlier in the sense that it was the site of an early monastic church, which were the targets of initial Viking plundering raids in the first phase of their activity in Ireland. Another anomaly in the documentary evidence is at *Mag Itha*, the site of which is unconfirmed, but which is mapped here along the River Finn. *Mag Itha* was a significant location in early medieval, even prehistoric, Donegal, and alongside other sites of royalty or lordship such as at *Cenn Magair*, Carrickabraghy and Grianán of Aileach, it is logical that Vikings would encounter Irish native leadership in their own bases. The documentary evidence suggests some degree of temporary settlement in the Cenél nEógain territory around Inishowen, following the alliance of Áed Findliath with the Dublin Vikings. His later routing of the Vikings across the northern territories may explain the abandonment of the sites, and

Conclusion

the leaving behind of archaeological evidence such as the hoards discussed above. Four hoards of Viking silver have been unearthed on the Inishowen Peninsula, at 'north-west Inishowen', Carrowmore, Roosky and Raphoe. This supports the possible evidence for Viking *longphort* camps on Lough Swilly and Lough Foyle. While some degree of temporary settlement took place in Donegal, Vikings were consistently pushed back by native Irish kings in the county and surrounding areas. Thus, Vikings could not muster enough power to establish towns in the way that they could in Dublin, Wexford, Waterford, Limerick and Cork.

Although the Vikings who came to Donegal seem to have been defeated and driven out, they left a permanent legacy. While never gaining enough power to establish long-lasting strongholds, Vikings clearly did assimilate into the county's social and political culture. This is most evident in language, surnames, place-names and folklore. Forgotten loanwords originating from Old Norse that survive in the Irish language are still spoken daily in Gaeltacht Dhún na nGall. Peaceful relations and intermarriage between Vikings and native Irish are reflected in personal names and family names associated with Co. Donegal, such as McManus, McAuley, Grimes, Higney, Reynolds, Sweeney and others. Old Norse influence on place-names was also significant and survives mainly in the coastal areas and islands. This coincides with the evidence that Vikings were experts of the seas and seamanship, dominating islands, fjords and bays. Perhaps, these areas of lesser development and small populations provided the conditions for Old Norse place-names to survive where Viking settlements once existed.

An intangible piece of evidence for Vikings in Co. Donegal, unaffected by social or geographical bounds, is folklore. A striking number of folktales in the county describe Vikings, usually as 'Danes', in a number of settings, but most particularly in association with tunnels, caves and forts in the landscape. The various denoted motivations for the 'Danes' to create these forts were for means of escape, hiding treasure and worship. We cannot say definitively if the Irish built souterrains for protection from Viking raids, or that there were Vikings making use of suspected souterrains, but we can certainly say that a legacy that associates the two exists in Donegal's oral culture. Is the reason no Viking settlements have been found in

Donegal that they adopted Irish habitation sites? The documentary evidence in Chapter 2 implies that the Viking presence in Donegal and the surrounding area was short-lived. Perhaps Vikings used Irish sites, which, upon their expulsion, never became *longphoirt* or fully fledged settlement sites. Various tales which describe Viking 'treasures' or graves may have some merit, as the Anglo-Saxon coin hoard was discovered at a location reputed to have stored hidden treasure, while the Roosky cashel was considered to be a 'Dane's Grave' by locals, long before the finding of a Viking silver hoard within its walls. For this reason, the Viking legacy in Donegal folklore must be granted significant merit.

To conclude, this study has shown that considerable evidence exists for Viking activity and at least temporary settlement in Donegal. The Irish name in itself, *Dún na nGall*, attests to Viking heritage, and it should be researched and embraced. This study, in combining material from a range of disciplines, has only scratched the surface of the available evidence. Further study must be undertaken on the extent of the evidence and, with time, more information may become available, and more artefacts uncovered. There is considerable interest among historians and archaeologists in Donegal, and the recent LiDAR survey of Dunree Head (possible *longphort* 'Cennrig') is potentially the first of many more archaeological investigations into Donegal's Viking history and heritage.[1]

Notes

ABBREVIATIONS

AClon	The Annals of Clonmacnoise, being annals of Ireland from the earliest period to AD1408, translated into English, AD1627 by Conell Mageoghagan, ed. and trans. Denis Murphy (Dublin, 1896).
AI	The Annals of Inisfallen (MS Rawlinson B503), ed. and trans. Seán Mac Airt (Dublin, 1951).
ALC	The Annals of Loch Cé: A chronicle of Irish affairs, from AD1014 to AD1590, 2 vols (London, 1871).
ARÉ (Irish) / AFM (English)	Annála ríoghachta Éireann: Annals of the kingdom of Ireland by the Four Masters, from the earliest times to the year 1616, ed. and trans. John O'Donovan. 2nd ed., 7 vols (Dublin, 1856).
AU	The Annals of Ulster (to AD1131), ed. and trans. Seán Mac Airt and Gearóid Mac Niocaill (Dublin, 1983).
CGG	Cogadh Gaedhel re Gallaibh: The war of the Gaedhil with the Gaill, or the Invasions of Ireland by the Danes and other Norsemen, ed. and trans. James Henthorn Todd (London, 1867).
CS	Chronicon Scotorum: A chronicle of Irish affairs, from the earliest times to AD1135: with a supplement, containing the events from 1141 to 1150, ed. and trans. William M. Hennessy (London, 1866) (also known as Chronicum Scotorum).
FAI	Fragmentary Annals of Ireland, ed. and trans. Joan Newlon Radner (Dublin, 1978).
FFÉ	Foras feasa ar Éirinn, 'The history of Ireland' by Geoffrey Keating, ed. and trans. David Comyn and Patrick S. Dineen (Cambridge, 1902).

INTRODUCTION

1 '*Dún na nGall*', Logainm.ie, www.logainm.ie/en/100013 (accessed 2 Nov. 2023).
2 *Foclóir Gaeilge-Bearla*, Ó Dónaill (1977), definitions online at Teanglann.ie, www.teanglann.ie/ga/fgb/gall, www.teanglann.ie/ga/fgb/d%C3%BAn (accessed 2 Nov. 2023).
3 'Viking', LEXICO, Oxford Dictionary Online www.lexico.com/en/definition/viking (accessed 30 Nov. 2023).
4 For more on Viking ancestry in Ireland and elsewhere, see Ashot Margaryan, D.J. Lawson and Maeve Sikora et al., 'Population genomics of the Viking world', *Nature*, 585 (2020), pp 390–6.
5 This has been disputed, see Ch. 2, 'Rathlin O'Birne'.
6 H.B. Clarke, 'The Vikings in Ireland: a historian's perspective', *Archaeology Ireland*, 9:3 (1995), p. 8.
7 Gareth Williams, quoted in Roger Atwood, 'The Vikings in Ireland', *Archaeology*, 68:2 (2015), p. 47.
8 Clarke, 'The Vikings in Ireland', p. 7.
9 Ibid.
10 Charles Doherty, 'Context: Ireland in the Viking Age', *History Ireland*, 22:2 (2014), p. 14.
11 Ibid.
12 Clarke, 'The Vikings in Ireland', p. 9.
13 S.P. Ó Ríordáin, 'Recent acquisitions from County Donegal in the National Museum', *Proceedings of the Royal Irish Academy*, 42 (1934/5), pp 145–91; Joseph Raftery, 'A hoard of Viking silver

bracelets from Co. Donegal', *Journal of the Royal Society of Antiquaries of Ireland*, 99 (1969), pp 133–43.
14 Harry Swan, *Twixt Foyle and Swilly: panorama of Ireland's wonderful peninsula: a guide book and conspectus of information relating to the barony of Inishown* (Dublin, 1949); Mabel Colhoun, 'Ballylin, Malin, Co. Donegal', *Ulster Journal of Archaeology*, 9 (1946), pp 84–6
15 James Graham-Campbell, 'The Viking-Age silver hoards of Ireland' in Bo Almqvist and David Greene (eds), *Proceedings of the Seventh Viking Congress* (Dublin, 1973), pp 31–74.
16 Michael Dolley, 'A neglected tenth-century coin-hoard from Donegal', *Ulster Journal of Archaeology*, 22 (1959), pp 56–8.
17 James Graham-Campbell, 'A Viking-Age silver hoard from near Raphoe, Co. Donegal' in Gearóid Mac Niocaill and Patrick Wallace (eds), *Keimelia: studies in medieval archaeology and history in memory of Tom Delaney* (Galway, 1988), pp 102–11.
18 Richard Warner, pers. comm.; Brian Lacy, *Archaeological survey of County Donegal: a description of the field antiquities of the county from the Mesolithic period to the 17th century AD* (Lifford, 1983), p. 66.
19 Michelle Comber et al., 'Tom Fanning's excavations at Rinnaraw Cashel, Portnablagh, Co. Donegal', *Proceedings of the Royal Irish Academy*, 106C (2006), pp 67–124.
20 Maeve Sikora, 'A hoard of Viking-Age silver ring-money from Lurgabrack, Horn Head, Co. Donegal', *Journal of the Royal Society of Antiquaries of Ireland*, 142 (2012), pp 191–6.
21 D.P. Dymond, *Archaeology and history: a plea for reconciliation* (London, 1974), p. 9.
22 Ibid.
23 Ibid., p. 16.
24 CELT Project online, www.ucc.ie/celt/publishd.html; Irish Script on Screen Project online, www.isos.dias.ie (accessed 12 Nov. 2023).
25 Brian Lacey, *Lug's forgotten Donegal kingdom: the archaeology, history and folklore of the Síl Lugdach of Cloghaneely* (Dublin, 2012), pp 48–51.
26 Joan Radner, 'Writing history: early Irish historiography and the significance of form', *Celtica*, 23 (1999), p. 313.
27 Ibid., p. 314.
28 Katharine Simms, *Medieval Gaelic sources* (Dublin, 2009), p. 57.
29 'Longphort', Electronic Dictionary of the Irish Language, www.dil.ie/search?q=longphort&search_in=headword (accessed 28 Nov. 2023).
30 'Marriages, 1852–1900', Donegal Genealogy, http://donegalgenealogy.com/clonmanymarriagebrideb.htm (accessed 28 Nov. 2023).
31 Diarmaid Ó Muirithe, 'The words we use', *Irish Times*, www.irishtimes.com/news/the-words-we-use-1.223880 (accessed 24 Nov. 2023).
32 Seán Mac Labhraí, 'Local placenames', *Before I forget ...: Journal of the Poyntzpass and District Local History Society*, 3 (1989), p. 15.
33 J.B. Arthurs, 'The Ulster Place-Name Society', *Ulster Journal of Archaeology*, 16 (1953), pp 104–5.
34 Nollaig Ó Muraíle, 'Some thoughts on matters onomastic', *Journal of the Galway Archaeological and Historical Society*, 53 (2001), p. 25.
35 Jan Tent, 'Approaches to research in toponymy', *Names*, 63 (2015), p. 65.

1. ARCHAEOLOGICAL EVIDENCE FOR VIKINGS IN CO. DONEGAL
1 For Viking-Age archaeology in Co. Donegal, see also Megan McAuley, '*Dún na nGall*: "Fort of the foreigners"?: archaeological evidence for Viking activity in medieval Donegal', *Donegal Annual*, 74 (2022).
2 Graham-Campbell, 'A Viking-Age silver hoard from near Raphoe', p. 104.
3 Ibid.
4 Graham-Campbell, 'The Viking-Age silver hoards of Ireland', p. 51n18. 'Penannular' means in the form of an incomplete ring.
5 Graham-Campbell, 'A Viking-Age silver hoard from near Raphoe', p. 105.
6 Ibid., p. 106.
7 Ibid., pp 105–6.
8 Dolley, 'A neglected tenth-century coin-hoard', p. 56.
9 Ibid.
10 Ibid., p. 57.
11 Ibid., p. 58.
12 Ibid., p. 57.

Notes to pages 16 to 29

13 Ibid.
14 Ibid., p. 58.
15 Graham-Campbell, 'A Viking-Age silver hoard from near Raphoe', p. 102.
16 Ibid.
17 Ibid., p. 103.
18 Ibid.
19 Ibid., p. 106.
20 James Graham-Campbell, 'The Viking-Age silver and gold hoards of Scandinavian character from Scotland', *Proceedings of the Society of Antiquaries of Scotland*, 107 (1976), pp 114–35.
21 Graham-Campbell, 'A Viking-Age silver hoard from near Raphoe', p. 106.
22 Ibid., p. 108.
23 Ibid.
24 Ibid.
25 Ibid.
26 Ó Ríordáin, 'Recent acquisitions', p. 174.
27 Ibid., p. 175.
28 Ibid.
29 Ibid., pp 175–6.
30 Ibid., p. 176.
31 Ibid., p. 177.
32 Ibid.
33 Ibid.
34 Ibid., pp 177–8.
35 Adolf Mahr, *Christian art in ancient Ireland* (New York, 1977), p. 54; Thomas Downing Kendrick, *A history of the Vikings* (New York, 1930), p. 208.
36 Ó Ríordáin, 'Recent acquisitions', p. 180.
37 Ibid.
38 Ibid., pp 180–1.
39 Ibid., p. 181.
40 Ibid.
41 Colm O'Brien et al., 'The early ecclesiastical complexes of Carrowmore and Clonca and their landscape context in Inishowen, County Donegal', *Ulster Journal of Archaeology*, 7 (2013), p. 148.
42 Raftery, 'A hoard of Viking silver bracelets from Co. Donegal', p. 133.
43 S.P. Ó Ríordáin, 'Lough Gur excavations: Carraig Aille and the "spectacles"', *Proceedings of the Royal Irish Academy*, 52 (1948), pp 39–111.
44 Raftery, 'A hoard of Viking silver bracelets from Co. Donegal', p. 135.
45 Ibid.
46 Michael Dolley and Joan Ingold, 'Viking-Age coin-hoards from Ireland and their relevance to Anglo-Saxon studies' in Michael Dolley (ed.), *Anglo-Saxon coins: studies presented to F.M. Stenton* (London, 1965), p. 260.
47 Sikora, 'A hoard of Viking-Age silver ring-money', p. 191.
48 Ibid.
49 Ibid., p. 192.
50 John Sheehan and Maeve Sikora, 'Lurgabrack, Co. Donegal: a Viking-Age hoard of Scoto-Scandinavian silver', *Journal of Irish Archaeology*, 28 (2013), p. 113.
51 Ibid., p. 104.
52 Sikora, 'A hoard of Viking-Age silver ring-money', p. 192.
53 Ibid., p. 193.
54 Richard Warner, 'Scottish silver arm-rings: an analysis of weights', *Proceedings of the Society of Antiquaries of Scotland*, 107 (1976), p. 136.
55 Sikora, 'A hoard of Viking-Age silver ring-money', p. 192.
56 Graham-Campbell, 'The Viking-Age silver and gold hoards'.
57 Sikora, 'A hoard of Viking-Age silver ring-money', p. 193.
58 Sheehan and Sikora, 'Lurgabrack, Co. Donegal', p. 110.
59 Ibid., pp 110–11.
60 Sikora, 'A hoard of Viking-Age silver ring-money', p. 193.
61 Ibid.
62 Lacy, *Archaeological survey*; Comber et al., 'Tom Fanning's excavations at Rinnaraw', p. 69.
63 Comber et al., 'Tom Fanning's excavations at Rinnaraw', p. 67.
64 Ibid., p. 71.
65 Ibid., pp 73–4.
66 Ibid., p. 73.
67 Ibid., pp 78–81.
68 Ibid., p. 84.
69 Ibid., pp 85–6.
70 Ibid., p. 106.
71 S.P. Ó Ríordáin and J.B. Foy, 'The excavation of Leacanabuaile Fort, Co. Kerry', *Journal of the Cork Historical and Archaeological Society*, 46 (1943), pp 85–99; C.J. Lynn, 'The excavation of Rathmullan, a raised rath and motte in Co. Down', *Ulster Journal of Archaeology*, 44/45 (1981), pp 65–171; James Graham-Campbell and C.E. Batey,

Vikings in Scotland (Edinburgh, 1998), pp 161–3.
72 Comber et al., 'Tom Fanning's excavations at Rinnaraw', pp 108–9.
73 Graham-Campbell, 'A Viking-Age silver hoard from near Raphoe', p. 103.
74 Graham-Campbell, 'The Viking-Age silver hoards', Appendix D, p. 71.
75 Ó Ríordáin, 'Recent acquisitions', p. 164.
76 G.H. Kinahan, 'Additional list of megalithic and other ancient structures, barony of Kilmacrenan, County Donegal', *Journal of the Royal Society of Antiquaries of Ireland*, 19 (1889), p. 281.
77 Ibid.
78 Lacy, *Archaeological survey*, p. 66.
79 Thomas Fanning, 'The Viking grave goods discovered near Larne, Co. Antrim, in 1840', *Journal of the Royal Society of Antiquaries of Ireland*, 100 (1970), p. 76.
80 Ó Ríordáin, 'Recent acquisitions', pp 182–3.
81 Tomás Ó Canann, 'Carraig an Dúnáin: probable Ua Canannáin inauguration site', *Journal of the Royal Society of Antiquaries of Ireland*, 133 (2003), p. 40.
82 Ibid.
83 Ibid.
84 Graham-Campbell, 'A Viking-Age silver hoard from near Raphoe', p. 106.

2. DOCUMENTARY EVIDENCE FOR VIKINGS IN CO. DONEGAL
1 F.J. Byrne, *Irish kings and high-kings* (Dublin, 2001), p. 40.
2 Doherty, 'Context', p. 15.
3 Byrne, *Irish kings and high-kings*, p. 40.
4 Ibid.
5 Donnchadh Ó Corráin, 'The Vikings in Scotland and Ireland in the ninth century', *Chronicon*, 2 (1998), no. 3, www.ucc.ie/research/chronicon/ocor2fra.htm (accessed 25 Nov. 2023), unpaginated.
6 Brian Lacey, pers. comm.
7 Clarke, 'The Vikings in Ireland', pp 8–9.
8 Annals of Ulster 833, henceforth AU.
9 Byrne, *Irish kings and high-kings*, pp 262–3.
10 Emer Purcell, 'Ninth-century Viking entries in the Irish annals: no "forty years" rest' in John Sheehan and Donnchadh Ó Corráin (eds), *The Viking Age: Ireland and the West* (Cork, 2005), pp 322–37.
11 Charles Doherty, 'The Vikings in Ireland: a review' in H.B. Clarke, Máire Ní Mhaonaigh and Raghnall Ó Floinn (eds), *Ireland and Scandinavia in the early Viking Age* (Dublin, 1998), p. 295.
12 Clarke, 'The Vikings in Ireland', p. 9.
13 Doherty, 'The Vikings in Ireland', p. 295.
14 Clare Downham, 'Viking camps in ninth-century Ireland: sources, locations and interactions', Academia.edu, www.academia.edu/15140025/Viking_Camps_in_Ninth-century_Ireland_Sources_Locations_and_Interactions (accessed 17 Mar. 2020), unpaginated.
15 Purcell, 'Ninth-century Viking entries', p. 322.
16 Edel Bhreathnach and Bernadette Cunningham, *Writing Irish history: the Four Masters and their world* (Bray, 2007), p. 106.
17 Donnchadh Ó Corráin, *Ireland before the Normans* (Dublin, 1972), pp 91–2, 109.
18 Donnchadh Ó Corráin, 'Nationality and kingship in pre-Norman Ireland' in T.W. Moody (ed.), *Nationality and the pursuit of national independence* (Belfast, 1978), pp 31–2.
19 Purcell, 'Ninth-century Viking entries', p. 322.
20 Downham, 'Viking camps in ninth-century Ireland'.
21 'Longphort', Electronic Dictionary of the Irish Language, online at www.dil.ie/search?q=longphort&search_in=headword (accessed 18 Nov. 2023), Annála Ríoghachta Éireann 1461, henceforth ARÉ.
22 Downham, 'Viking camps in ninth-century Ireland'.
23 For more on *Laithlinn*, see Mary Valante, 'Family relics and Viking kingship in Ireland', *Eolas: the Journal of the American Society of Irish Medieval Studies*, 6 (2013), pp 88–106; Colmán Etchingham, '*Laithlinn*, "Fair Foreigners" and "Dark Foreigners": the identity and provenance of Vikings in ninth-century Ireland' in John Sheehan and Donnchadh Ó Corráin (eds), *The Viking Age: Ireland and the West* (Dublin, 2005), pp 80–8; Colmán Etchingham, 'The location of historical *Laithlinn/Lochla(i)nn*: Scotland or

Scandinavia?' in Mícheál Ó Flaithearta (ed.), *Proceedings of the Seventh Symposium of Societas Celtologica Nordica* (Uppsala, 2007), pp 11–37.
24 Ó Corráin, 'The Vikings in Scotland and Ireland'.
25 Brian Lacey, 'The ringed cross at Ray, Co. Donegal: context and date', *Journal of Irish Archaeology*, 25 (2016), p. 63.
26 Ibid., p. 62.
27 *Cogadh Gaedhel re Gallaibh* 838, henceforth CGG.
28 AU 837.
29 AU 842.
30 AFM 841; AClon 839.
31 AU 842.
32 Downham, 'Viking camps in ninth-century Ireland'.
33 Brian Lacey, pers. comm.
34 Siobhan McDermott, QUB Centre for Archaeological Fieldwork, 'Geophysical survey report no. 35', p. 3.
35 Thomas McErlean, Rosemary McConkey and Wes Forsythe, *Strangford Lough: an archaeological survey of a maritime landscape* (Newtownards, 2002), p. 79.
36 Lenore Fischer, 'A county by county reference to Viking activities in Ireland', www.vikingage.mic.ul.ie/pdfs/c7_viking-activity-in-ireland-by-county-in-annals (accessed 13 Nov. 2023).
37 P.J. Bracken, 'The Vikings in Ulaid' (MPhil., University College Cork, 2020), p. 40.
38 Ibid.
39 Ibid.
40 Clare Downham, 'Coastal communities and diaspora identities in Viking-Age Ireland' in James Barrett and Sarah Gibbon (eds), *Maritime societies of the Viking and medieval world* (Leeds, 2015), p. 374.
41 AU 845; CS 845.
42 Brian Lacey, *Cénel Conaill and the Donegal kingdoms, AD500–800* (Dublin, 2006), p. 43.
43 Ó Corráin, *Ireland before the Normans*, p. 17.
44 Lacey, *Lug's forgotten Donegal kingdom*, p. 45.
45 Ó Corráin, 'The Vikings in Scotland and Ireland'.
46 *Fragmentary Annals* 247 (856), henceforth FAI.
47 AU 856.
48 Ibid.
49 Ó Corráin, 'The Vikings in Scotland and Ireland'.
50 AU 861; AU 862; FAI 861; AFM 860.
51 AFM 864; AClon 864.
52 AU 866.
53 Bracken, 'The Vikings in Ulaid', p. 42.
54 Downham, 'Viking camps in ninth-century Ireland'.
55 Emer Purcell and John Sheehan, 'Viking Dublin: enmities, alliances and the cold gleam of silver' in D.M. Hadley and Letty Ten Harkel (eds), *Everyday life in Viking 'towns': social approaches to Viking-Age towns in Ireland and England, c.850–1100* (Oxford, 2013), p. 42.
56 Stephen Harrison, 'Review of *The kings of Aileach and the Vikings, AD800–1060*, by Darren McGettigan', *English Historical Review*, 137 (2022), p. 576.
57 AU 871.
58 Downham, 'Viking camps in ninth-century Ireland'.
59 AU 866.
60 AU 895; AFM 893. AU refers to the 'foreigners of Áth Cliath' not 'of Lough Foyle'. This raises questions about both entries.
61 Downham, 'Viking camps in ninth-century Ireland'.
62 Lacey, *Lug's forgotten Donegal kingdom*, p. 32.
63 Katharine Simms, 'The Donegal poems in the Book of Fenagh', *Ériu*, 58 (2008), p. 40.
64 Ó Corráin, 'Nationality and kingship in pre-Norman Ireland', p. 32.
65 Lacey, *Lug's forgotten Donegal kingdom*, p. 48.
66 AFM 901.
67 Dobbs, 'A poem ascribed to Flann Mac Lonáin', *Ériu*, 17 (1995), p. 23.
68 Lacey, *Lug's forgotten Donegal kingdom*, p. 48.
69 Dobbs, 'A poem ascribed to Flann Mac Lonáin', p. 23.
70 Ibid., p. 26.
71 Dobbs, 'A poem ascribed to Flann Mac Lonáin', p. 31; ARÉ 915; AFM 917 describes the battle but does not mention Gartnel.
72 Lacey, *Lug's forgotten Donegal kingdom*, p. 48.

73 CS 904.
74 AFM 900.
75 John O'Donovan, *Annála ríoghachta Éireann: Annals of the kingdom of Ireland, by the Four Masters, from the earliest period to the year 1616*, 1 (Dublin, 1856), p. 560.
76 Ibid., p. 284.
77 Richard Warner, 'Ireland, Ulster and Scotland in the earlier Iron Age' in A. O'Connor and D.V. Clarke (eds), *From the Stone-Age to the Forty-Five* (Edinburgh, 1983), p. 178.
78 Henry Morris, 'The circuit of Ireland by Muirchertach na gCochall gCroiceann, AD941', *Journal of the Royal Society of Antiquaries of Ireland*, 66 (1936), p. 29.
79 James Hogan, 'Irish law of kingship, with special reference to Ailech and Cenel Eoghain', *Proceedings of the Royal Irish Academy*, 6 (1932), pp 201–2.
80 Brian Lacey, 'The Grianán of Aileach: a note on its identification', *Journal of the Royal Society of Antiquaries of Ireland*, 131 (2001), p. 146.
81 Ibid., pp 146–7.
82 Lacey, *Lug's forgotten Donegal kingdom*, p. 111.
83 AU 921.
84 AU 921; AFM 919.
85 Raghnall Ó Floinn, 'Sandhills, silver and shrines: fine metalwork of the medieval period from Donegal' in William Nolan, Liam Ronayne and Mairead Dunlevy (eds), *Donegal history and society: interdisciplinary essays on the history of an Irish county* (Dublin, 1995), p. 103.
86 John Sheehan, 'The longphort in Viking-Age Ireland', *Acta Archaeologica*, 79 (2008), p. 292.
87 Clare Downham, 'Viking settlements in Ireland before 1014' in Jón Vidar Sigurdsson and Timothy Bolton (eds), *Celtic-Norse relationships in the Irish Sea in the Middle Ages, 800–1200* (Leiden, 2013), p. 9.
88 Lacy, *Archaeological survey*, p. 66.
89 AU 921.
90 AFM 937; AU 939.
91 CS 943.
92 CS 943.
93 AFM 941.
94 'Eglinton, Derry', PlacenamesNI.org, www.placenamesni.org/resultdetails.php?entry=524 (accessed 18 Nov. 2023).
95 Brian Lacey, pers. comm.
96 Paul Walsh, 'The monastic settlement on Rathlin O'Birne Island, County Donegal', *Journal of the Royal Society of Antiquaries of Ireland*, 113 (1983), p. 54.
97 Ludwig Bieler, *The Patrician texts in the Book of Armagh* (Dublin, 1979), p. 140.
98 Walsh, 'The monastic settlement', p. 64.
99 Brian Lacey, pers. comm.
100 Most recently, in 2022, a rare Viking female burial was discovered on Rathlin Island. See 'Rathlin burial', National Museums NI, www.nationalmuseumsni.org/collections/rathlin-burial (23 Jan. 2024).
101 Tomás Ó Cannan, 'The Annals of Inisfallen: an independent witness to northern events', *Journal of the Cork Historical and Archaeological Society*, 113 (2008), p. 32.
102 Lacey and Mac Gairbheá, forthcoming, 2024.
103 Sean Beattie, pers. comm.; *The book of Inishtrahull* (Culdaff, 1992).
104 Sean Beattie, pers. comm.; *The book of Inishtrahull* (Culdaff, 1992).
105 Sheehan, 'The longphort in Viking-Age Ireland', p. 292.
106 Graham-Campbell, 'A Viking-Age silver hoard from near Raphoe', pp 109–10.

3. VIKING LEGACIES IN DONEGAL

1 Darren McGettigan, *The kings of Ailech and the Vikings, AD800–1060* (Dublin, 2020).
2 Doherty, 'The Vikings in Ireland: a review', p. 288.
3 'Donegal Gaeltacht', Údarás na Gaeltachta, www.udaras.ie/en/an-ghaeilge-an-ghaeltacht/an-ghaeltacht/dun-na-ngall (accessed 1 Dec. 2023).
4 David Greene, 'The influence of Scandinavian on Irish' in Bo Almqvist and David Greene (eds), *Proceedings of the Seventh Viking Congress* (Dundalk, 1973), p. 76.
5 R.W. McDonald, 'Dynamics of identity: Norse loanword-borrowers in Ireland and Scotland, and linguistic evidence of urbanization', *Eolas: The Journal of the American Society of Irish Medieval Studies*, 11 (2018), p. 2.

Notes to pages 50 to 59

6. Donnchadh Ó Corráin, 'Ireland, Wales, Man and the Hebrides' in Peter Sawyer (ed.), *The Oxford illustrated history of the Vikings* (Oxford, 1997), p. 104; Magne Oftedal, 'On the frequency of Norse loanwords in Scottish Gaelic', *Scottish Gaelic Studies*, 9 (1961–2), p. 119; David Greene, 'The influence of Scandinavian on Irish' in Bo Almqvist and David Greene (eds), *Proceedings of the Seventh Viking Congress* (Dublin, 1976), p. 80.
7. McDonald, 'Dynamics of identity', pp 2–3.
8. Ibid., p. 3
9. Ibid., pp 5–6.
10. Donnchadh Ó Corráin, 'The Vikings in Ireland' in A.-C. Larsen (ed.), *The Vikings in Ireland* (Roskilde, 2001), p. 27.
11. Greene, 'The influence of Scandinavian on Irish', p. 76
12. Ibid., pp 76–7.
13. Ibid., p. 77.
14. Colmán Etchingham, *Viking raids on Irish church settlements in the ninth century* (Maynooth, 1996), pp 49–53.
15. 'Gall', Teanglann.ie www.teanglann.ie/en/fgb/gall (accessed 1 Dec. 2023).
16. Greene, 'The influence of Scandinavian on Irish', p. 78.
17. McDonald, 'Dynamics of identity', pp 11–13.
18. Greene, 'The influence of Scandinavian on Irish', p. 82.
19. Ibid., p. 79.
20. Mary Valante, *The Vikings in Ireland: settlement, trade and urbanization* (Dublin, 2008), p. 53.
21. McGettigan, *The kings of Ailech*, p. 88.
22. Etchingham, *Viking raids on Irish church settlements*, p. 55.
23. Valante, *The Vikings in Ireland*, p. 92.
24. Ibid., p. 94.
25. Kenneth Jackson, 'The Celtic languages during the Viking period' in Brian Ó Cuív (ed.), *The impact of the Scandinavian invasions on the Celtic-speaking peoples, c.800–1100AD* (Dublin, 1975), pp 5–10.
26. John O'Donovan, 'Origin and meanings of Irish family names', *Irish Penny Journal*, 1:46 (1841), p. 365.
27. Gillian Fellows-Jensen, 'Nordic names and loanwords in Ireland' in

A.-C. Larsen (ed.), *The Vikings in Ireland* (Roskilde, 2001), p. 111.
28. Ó Muraíle, 'Some thoughts', p. 40.
29. John Grenham, 'Irish roots: Viking surnames', *Irish Times*, www.irishtimes.com/culture/heritage/irish-roots-viking-surnames-1.2392951 (accessed 11 May 2020).
30. Fergus Mac Giolla Easpaig, 'The Gaelic families of Donegal' in William Nolan, Liam Ronayne and Mairead Dunlevy (eds), *Donegal: history and society* (Dublin, 1995), p. 773.
31. Greene, 'The influence of Scandinavian on Irish', p. 78.
32. Ibid.
33. Carl Marstrander, *Bidrag til det norske sprogs historie I Irland* (Oslo, 1915), p. 110.
34. Magne Oftedal, 'The village names of Lewis in the Outer Hebrides', *Norsk Tidsskrift for Sprogvidenskap*, xvii (1954), p. 388.
35. Greene, 'The influence of Scandinavian on Irish', p. 78.
36. Mac Giolla Easpaig, 'The Gaelic families of Donegal', p. 762.
37. Ibid., pp 778–9.
38. Arthurs, 'The Ulster Place-Name Society', pp 104–5.
39. Ibid.
40. Fellows-Jensen, 'Nordic names and loanwords in Ireland', p. 107.
41. Ibid., pp 107–10.
42. Ibid.
43. Patrick Weston Joyce, *A pocket guide to Irish place-names* (Belfast, 2006), p. 59.
44. Patrick McKay, *A dictionary of Ulster place-names* (2nd edn, Belfast, 2009), p. 58.
45. Donal Mac Giolla Easpaig, 'Place-names and early settlement in County Donegal' in William Nolan, Liam Ronayne and Mairead Dunlevy (eds), *Donegal: history and society* (Dublin, 1995), pp 161–2.
46. Ibid., p. 162.
47. Ó Canann, 'Carraig an Dúnáin', p. 40.
48. Ó Muraíle, 'Some thoughts', p. 39.
49. Sean Beattie, pers. comm.; *The book of Inistrahull* (Culdaff, 1992).
50. 'Malin Head', Donegal County Council, www.donegalcoco.ie/media/donegalcountyc/archives/Malin%20Head%20booklet%20PDF.pdf (accessed 1 Dec. 2023).

51 Ó Floinn, 'Sandhills, silver and shrines', p. 103.
52 'Clonmany marriages', Donegal Genealogy, http://donegalgenealogy.com/clonmanymarriages.htm (accessed 11 Nov. 2023).
53 James MacGrady, 'Irish surnames: their past and present forms', *Ulster Journal of Archaeology*, 1 (1853), p. 117.
54 'Drumholm', Logainm.ie www.logainm.ie/en/785?s=drumholm (accessed 1 Dec. 2023).
55 'Drumholm', collected by Jim Travers www.duchas.ie/en/cbes/4428274/4390717/4458325 (accessed 1 Dec. 2023). 'Drumholm', collected by Mary Langan www.duchas.ie/en/cbes/4428267/4390040/4478812 (accessed 1 Dec. 2023).
56 'A discovery', collected by Una Begley www.duchas.ie/en/cbes/4428268/4390115/4478889 (accessed 1 Dec. 2023).
57 'Drumholm', collected by Jim Travers www.duchas.ie/en/cbes/4428274/4390717/4458325 (accessed 1 Dec. 2023).
58 'Earthen Forts', collected by Susan Mary Irwin www.duchas.ie/en/cbes/4428255/4388873/4477401 (accessed 1 Dec. 2023).
59 Untitled, collected by John Doherty www.duchas.ie/en/cbes/4428403/4404898/4514947 (accessed 1 Dec. 2023).
60 'Seanfhoirgnithe', collected by Winnie Harkin www.duchas.ie/en/cbes/4493637/4406352/4515582 (accessed 1 Dec. 2023).
61 Graham-Campbell, 'The Viking-Age silver hoards of Ireland', Appendix D, p. 71.
62 Margareta Weidhagen-Hallerdt, 'A possible ringfort from the late Viking period in Helsingborg', *Current Swedish Archaeology*, 17 (2009), p. 187.
63 Thomas Johnson Westropp, 'The ancient forts of Ireland: being a contribution towards our knowledge of their types, affinities and structural features (plates LII to LIX)', *Transactions of the Royal Irish Academy*, 31 (1896), p. 583.
64 Lacy, *Archaeological survey*, p. 152.
65 'Castlecommon', collected by Mary O'Donnell www.duchas.ie/en/cbes/4428304/4393075/4477842 (accessed 1 Dec. 2023).
66 'The stone of the hidden treasure', collected by P. McCloskey www.duchas.ie/en/cbes/4428298/4392561/4476017 (accessed 1 Dec. 2023).
67 'Ráthanna agus Liosanna', collected by Seorsamh Mac Aoidh www.duchas.ie/en/cbes/5260484/5258558/5266127 (accessed 1 Dec. 2023).
68 'Cistí Óir i bhFolach', collected by Alphonsus Crossan www.duchas.ie/en/cbes/4493636/4406161/4524847 (accessed 1 Dec. 2023).
69 'Hidden Treasures', collected by Eileen McBrearty www.duchas.ie/en/cbes/4428277/4391308/4462498 (accessed 1 Dec. 2023).
70 Untitled, unknown collector www.duchas.ie/en/cbes/4428255/4388840 (accessed 1 Dec. 2023).
71 Doherty, 'The Viking impact upon Ireland', p. 70.
72 Chris Synnott, 'A survey of published reasons for burying butter in bogs', *Ulster Journal of Archaeology*, 69 (2010), p. 147.
73 'Hidden treasure', collected by Leonard Bovaird www.duchas.ie/en/cbes/4493783/4419962/4535854 (accessed 1 Dec. 2023).
74 'Forts', collected by Mary McCafferty www.duchas.ie/en/cbes/4428274/4390716/4458324 (accessed 1 Dec. 2023).
75 'Cistí Óir i bhFolach', collected by Frances MacNulty www.duchas.ie/en/cbes/4493636/4406165/4524968 (accessed 1 Dec. 2023).
76 'Bones found this week', collected by Evelyn Harron www.duchas.ie/en/cbes/4428269/4390236/4479126 (accessed 1 Dec. 2023).
77 Ibid.
78 Ibid.
79 Synnott, 'A survey of published reasons', p. 144.
80 Richard Warner, 'The Irish souterrains and their background' in H. Crawford (ed.), *Subterranean Britain* (London, 1979), pp 120–8.

81 'Caves', collected by Pearl Hunter www.duchas.ie/en/cbes/4493634/4406114/4519159 (accessed 1 Dec. 2023).
82 Ibid.
83 'A Dane's cave and graveyard', collected by David John Bovaird www.duchas.ie/en/cbes/4428404/4404961/4515145 (accessed 1 Dec. 2023).
84 Jürg Glauser, Pernille Hermann and S.A. Mitchell (eds), *Handbook of pre-modern Nordic memory studies: interdisciplinary approaches* (Berlin, 2018).
85 'Ale, brewing and Fulacht Fiadh: *Archaeology Ireland*', Moore Group www.mooregroup.ie/2007/10/the-archaeology-ireland-article (accessed 17 Nov. 2023).

CONCLUSION

1 'Dunrioga: a royal fort standing on Cennrig, a royal headland', Donegal Live www.donegallive.ie/news/inishowen/588314/dunrioga-a-royal-fort-standing-on-cennrig-a-royal-headland.html (accessed 14 Nov. 2023).

Index

Aileach, Co. Donegal 39, 43–5, 68
Anglo-Saxon coins 9, 14, 16–17, 31, 64, 70
Annals of the Four Masters 10, 34, 37, 41, 43–5
Annals of Ulster 10, 34–41, 55
Ard na scéla, a mheic na ccuach 10, 41–3
Assaroe, Co. Donegal 36, 67–8

Bóruma, Brian 8–9, 54
Bøstrand hoard 19
Burt, Co. Donegal 9, 16, 25, 31, 43, 64, 67

Carrickabraghy, Co. Donegal 10, 41–3, 68
Carrowmore, Co. Donegal 9, 14–15, 19–22, 25, 31, 60, 63, 69, Figs 3, 4
Cenél Conaill dynasty 36, 38, 42, 46
Cenél nEógain dynasty 38–47, 53–7, 68
Chronicon Scotorum 10, 43
Clondahorky, Co. Donegal 14, 29, 62
Clontarf, Battle of 8, 34
Cogadh Gaedhel re Gallaibh 8, 33–4, 36
Cuerdale hoard 20

Danes 7, 9, 30, 51, 58, 61–6, 69–70, Table 3
Derry, County 33, 41, 43, 46
Doonan Rock 30–1, 58
Drontheim, sailing boat (o/w Greencastle yawl) 49
Drumholm, Co. Donegal 61–2
Dublin 7–10, 31, 33–5, 39–40, 48–50, 53–5, 57, 59, 68–9
Dunree Head, Co. Donegal 44, 70

Éichnechán, lord of Fanad 10–11, 41–3

Findliath, Áed 39–41, 53–5, 68
'Fort of the Foreigners' 7, 13, 31, 58, 60
Fragmentary Annals of Ireland 34, 54

Gall-Ghaedhil, gallowglasses 38–9, 53–4, 56–7
Glúndub mac Áeda, Niall 43
Grimestad hoard 18–19

Hiberno-Norse 15, 18–19, 26, 31, 34, 51–5

Inishbofin, Co. Donegal 7, 30, 33, 47
Inishbofin, Co. Galway 7, 33, 47
Inishowen, Co. Donegal 9, 12, 14–15, 17, 19, 22, 25, 31, 37, 42–7, 49, 56, 60, 62, 67–9, Fig. 1
Inishmurray, Co. Sligo 7, 33, 46–7
Inishtrahull, Co. Donegal 47, 59
Ívar, Viking king of Dublin (o/w Ímar) 53–4

Kinnegar, Co. Donegal 9, 14, 30, 37, 65
Kinnaweer, Co. Donegal 35, 42, 44–5

Laithlinn 35, 52, 56
Liss, Co. Donegal 14, 29
Lochlann 35, 52, 56, 61
Lough Foyle 19, 37, 39–41, 44–6, 64, 67, 69
Lough Swilly 16, 36–8, 40, 43–4, 62, 67, 69
Lurgabrack, Co. Donegal 14, 24–6, 31, 63, 65, 67, Fig. 6

Mac Lónain, Flann 10, 41–2
Mac Néill, Muichertach 45
Mag Itha, Co. Donegal 38, 68
Muff, Co. Donegal 45–6

Norse loanwords 50–3, 69, Table 1
Norse–Gael political alliance 34, 39–40, 43, 49, 53–5, 68
Northern Uí Néill 33, 37, 41, 43–4, 53, 55, 62

Óláfr, Viking king of Dublin (o/w Amlaíb) 33, 39–40, 53–4
Orkney Islands, Scotland 10, 14, 29

Raphoe, Co. Donegal 9, 14–15, 17–19, 24–6, 31, 60, 69, Fig. 2
Rathlin Island, Co. Antrim 7, 33, 36, 46, 47
Rathlin O'Birne, Co. Donegal 33, 36, 46, 47, 59
Rinnaraw, Co. Donegal 9–10, 14, 27–9, 31, 67, Fig. 7
Roosky, Co. Donegal 9, 14–15, 22–5, 31, 60, 63, 69–70, Fig. 5

Scotland 7, 9, 18, 25–7, 29–30, 32, 35–6, 39–40, 52, 54
Sechnaill, Mael 39–40, 53
Sheephaven Bay, Co. Donegal 9, 27, 59, 67
Skaill hoard 25

Tara, Co. Meath 34, 39, 45
þing, assembly mound 31

Ua Canannáin dynasty 30, 45–6
Ua Canannáin, Ruairí 45–6, 54

Viking graves 19, 30, 43, 47, 59, 61, 65–6, 70
Viking homelands 9, 33, 52
Viking place-names 9, 12, 37, 47–9, 53, 57–60, 66–9, Fig. 8, Table 2
Viking settlement phases 8, 11, 13, 22, 33, 36, 68
Viking towns 8–9, 32, 40, 51